Cover design by Mark Roos, The Netherlands

Anxiety – Deal with it! What works, when and why©

By Yvonne Bates

ISBN: 9781092581691

Other books by Yvonne Bates

Ethically Challenged Professions: enabling innovation and diversity in psychotherapy and counselling

Editors: Yvonne Bates and Richard House (2003)

PCCS Books, Ross on Wye, United Kingdom
ISBN 1 898059 61 6

Shouldn't I Be Feeling Better by Now? Client Views of Therapy

Editor: Yvonne Bates (2006)

Palgrave Macmillan, Basingstoke, United Kingdom and New York, USA
ISBN 1 4039 4740 6

Assisted Self-Help

With the best will in the world, it's sometimes hard to get everything you could out of a self-help book. For that reason, the author of this book offers a self-help workshop to help you put everything you've learned from the book into practice. It includes six one-hour Skype™ or telephone-based one-to-one coaching sessions.

Please see anxiety-self-help.co.uk for more details.

Anxiety – Deal with it!
What works, when and why

Contents

INTRODUCTION

Anxiety is an epidemic in modern society. Studies show that up to 33.7% of the population suffer from anxiety "disorders" at some point during their life[1]. So, if you have anxiety, you are certainly not alone. There has been so much written, studied and said on the subject of anxiety that you will be forgiven for thinking there's nothing more to say. However, I believe that there are three fundamental mistakes that underpin pretty much every single approach to anxiety that I have ever come across. The first is that anxiety is a state of mind, that it is the same as worrying, or an unease about something or several things. It is not. *It is a physical state that can be brought on by a number of things, of which worries are just one.* The second mistake is the assumption that if you do have a worry, that it is the cause of your anxiety. This is also wrong, because in *many cases the worry is a symptom of the anxiety, not the cause.* And the third mistake is that anxiety is always the same thing, and that it should always be treated in the same way. There are so many possible approaches to dealing with anxiety, some of which we find are more helpful than others. You might have found an approach that really works for you, but then find it lets you down on some occasions. The reason no one technique has ever emerged as

---

[1] See https://www.ncbi.nlm.nih.gov/pmc/articles/PMC4610617/

clearly the best way to treat anxiety is that there are many types of anxiety. *If we don't know what type we're dealing with, we're just employing a scattergun* approach when we apply our solutions.

This book will identify *categories* of techniques, and when and where each category should be used. It will teach you to *diagnose* your anxiety in a methodical, logical and targeted way. You will be able to work on the real cause of a *bout of anxiety* and apply the right kind of techniques to manage it. You'll be able to identify the reasons why you are *more prone to anxiety* than the next person and apply the right kind of technique to reducing that proneness. And you will learn to avoid a lot of anxiety altogether by *developing healthy habits* and *recognising the warning signs* and dealing with them before they lead to the kind of misery that anxiety can cause.

I have over a quarter of a century's experience as a person-centred therapist and have helped many clients who suffer with anxiety. I have struggled with anxiety myself for about the same length of time (I'm sure that's a coincidence though!) and was born to an anxious mother who exposed me to this affliction from a very early age. None of these things make me the world's expert, but I've picked up a lot of useful and not-so-useful ideas along the way. By developing the new approach I'm presenting in this book, I've certainly made some progress with my own anxiety, so I'm confident it can help with yours as well.

The book is perhaps at times more orientated toward the person who gets anxious about a number of things, rather than people with very specific anxieties. That's probably just the assumption I had in my head when writing, because it's the way I am myself. However, I believe that the book will be just as useful for dealing with specific anxieties, there just may be a few paragraphs and sections that you can skip to get to where you need to be.

This book is purely about anxiety, and not about depression. I think it's important to separate them, because they are two very different beasts. Depression tends to be a *constant state*, whereas anxiety, by nature, happens in *bouts*. Usually depression involves feeling *numb, detached and shut down*, whereas anxiety usually involves *heightened emotions and feeling hyper and exposed*. The thought patterns associated with depression often revolve around the *past and present*, whereas the thought patterns associated with anxiety are always about what is going to happen in the *future*. The medical community tends often to lump them together and diagnose people with both, and I am not at all sure this is helpful when it comes to treatment. You might "feel depressed" if you have ongoing problems with anxiety, but that is not the same as clinical depression, it's a natural response to having to deal with your condition. So, I hope you'll find that by reducing your anxiety using the techniques in this book, you will find that that feeling of depression will be lifted too.

One last thing before we begin – don't let the book cause you anxiety. There are a lot of exercises and things to learn, which could seem daunting. If you're struggling with anxiety right now, even just reading a book might feel like a pressure. If so, it's fine to just dip. Hopefully, if nothing else, the book is a gold mine full of nuggets that can help you to combat your anxiety.

Chapter 1. WHAT IS ANXIETY?

In this chapter:
- We'll talk about what anxiety really is, and how even the dictionary definitions are misleading and unhelpful
- We'll look at our primitive "fight-or-flight" mechanism, and how it works differently for different people
- We'll map out our approach to dealing with anxiety based on our new understanding of what it is.

Redefining Anxiety

Nobody has the solution to anxiety, because there is not one solution. Anxiety takes many forms and has many reasons and causes. Different solutions will work for different types of anxiety, but none will work for all types, and none will cure you completely. In fact, you'd be in trouble if you were cured completely, because anxiety, when it's appropriate and not out of control, is a *necessary part of human instinct*. In this book I will help you to look at anxiety differently, to see the different types and causes, and to tailor techniques that will help you to reduce the type of anxiety that is bothering you and that has made you pick up the book.

What is anxiety? It sounds like an obvious place to start, but in fact I think it's a really important question. We all think of anxiety as worrying, fretting, or panicking. The Oxford English Dictionary describes it as "A feeling of worry, nervousness, or unease about something with an uncertain outcome." And Merriam Webster's definition is "extreme uneasiness of mind or brooding fear about some contingency". But those of us who suffer from anxiety – well, most of us at least – sometimes don't even know why we're anxious. We can even find ourselves looking for things – "what am I anxious about? Something's bothering me, but I can't think what it is!" Sometimes in fact we are experiencing anxiety without even knowing we are ... we might have terrible backache, nausea, headache, tension, IBS, a lumpy throat ... they are all symptoms of anxiety, but there isn't necessarily a worry that has caused them or that goes with them.

I'm going to start by suggesting that we throw out these dictionary definitions and replace them with one of our own: *anxiety is the state of being in fight-or-flight mode.* What does this mean? Well, anxiety is a part of the survival mechanism that is needed for just about every creature in the animal kingdom. There are only two states that a human's (or an animal's) nervous system can be in: the normal, go-about-your-business state, or fight-or-flight[2], where you're on alert to respond to a threat. That is what being anxious is, in physical terms. If you're not in one of these states, you're in the other.

Type 1, Type 2 and Type 3 Anxiety

Take an animal such as the wildebeest (or gnu), the animal with the most natural predators in the world. She might be lazing around in the African sunshine, having just had a lovely meal. Her body is digesting her food, absorbing all the nutrients. Her heart rate is slow, allowing her to rest, relax and recuperate. She might even be contemplating a little romance.

---

[2] For the scientific minded, the fight-or-flight response vs. normal response is the activation of the sympathetic nervous system as opposed to the parasympathetic nervous system, both complementary elements of the autonomic nervous system. As Wikipedia says "The parasympathetic system is responsible for stimulation of "rest-and-digest" or "feed and breed" activities that occur when the body is at rest, especially after eating, including sexual arousal, salivation, lacrimation (tears), urination, digestion and defecation. Its action is described as being complementary to that of the sympathetic nervous system, which is responsible for stimulating activities associated with the fight-or-flight response."
The fight-or-flight response occurs at least partially through activation of a part of the brain known as the "amygdala", which is an almond shaped group of nuclei (there are usually two).
In technical terms, if these amygdalae are triggered too often, or too easily, for whatever reason (chemical, thinking patterns, genetic predisposition), then we will find ourselves in a consistently anxious fight-or-flight state.

Suddenly, she hears a sound in the bushes nearby. The instincts that have kept her species from extinction for centuries tell her, this could be a threat. She goes into fight-or-flight mode. The digestion process is put on hold. The heart rate increases to pump blood quicker to the organs required for defending herself (fight) – or running away (flight) – the limbs, muscles, eyes, ears. She is fully alert. In wildebeest terms, she could be described as anxious. *It's not a thought process, it's an instinct.* It's a good thing, it can save her life, it can keep her safe. Let's call this normal response to a threat **Type 1 Anxiety**.

But imagine a wildebeest who hears every single rustle of a leaf or buzzing of a fly as a threat. She would be constantly in fight-or-flight mode, so she wouldn't be spending long enough in go-about-your-business mode. She'd not be able to sleep properly, she would have digestion problems, probably along with all sorts of muscular disorders, because her muscles would always be tensed up ready for the fight or the flight and never in rest and recovery mode. Not only would this poor wildebeest be pretty miserable, assuming wildebeest have emotions like that, but ironically, she'd be more at risk of a real predator than the first wildebeest, because she'd probably be worn out from being in fight-or-flight all the time. **Let's call this Type 2 Anxiety**.

That second wildebeest is me, and if you're reading this book, I guess it is probably you as well, whether it's in specific situations, or generally. And I imagine, like me, you don't want to be like that. You want to be like the first wildebeest. Now, I've read many times that the trick is to distinguish between a real threat, and a perceived threat. Anxious people, or worriers, worry about things that might not happen. Those annoying so-laid-back-they're-horizontal folks say "you should only worry about it if it happens. Otherwise it's wasted energy." But that's not true, is it? Let's say there's wildebeest number 3, who hears that noise in the bushes ... but she doesn't go into fight-or-flight until it is confirmed that it is, in fact, a lion bounding towards her with her jaw open. She'll be too late won't she? The whole idea of fight-or-flight mode is to *prepare* us for action. You can't only worry about things if they happen. If they happen, it's already too late to be worrying! This would be an example of **Type 3 Anxiety** – and these type 3 people also exist – where the fight-or-flight response isn't triggered enough. So, worrying or anxiety is valuable. Do not try to get rid of it.

The fact is that, like the second wildebeest, for some reason, in Type 2 Anxiety (1) our fight-or-flight response gets triggered too often and/or too easily, (2) we go into a higher alert mode than is appropriate and/or (3) we stay in fight-or-flight longer than we should. These processes are all governed by a complex series of brain mechanisms and chemicals. It's not about worries and thoughts. *It's an involuntary physical response, an animal instinct, that is over sensitive, just like some people cry more easily than others, or sweat more.*

So, we can see that telling someone (or yourself) not to worry is like telling someone not to cry, or not to sweat. What we have to do is to understand what the triggers are, so we can be in fight-or-flight less and give ourselves far more time in go-about-your-business mode. Otherwise, we are going to make ourselves very unhappy and unhealthy. We don't want to be cured of anxiety, but we need to bring it back to a sensible level. We want to get closer to Type 1 Anxiety.

Horses for Courses

Of course, in our battle against anxiety, we need effective weapons. The measures, or techniques, that we put in place fall into different categories. Each is good for certain types of anxiety and/or certain reasons for our proneness to anxiety. Imagine that anxiety was a backache. You have a backache and want it to go away. You might try taking a pain killer. It works. But the next time you have a backache, you take the same painkiller, and it doesn't work. You wonder why it doesn't work. Someone suggests you try osteopathy. But that doesn't seem to work either. So you try anti-inflammatories, they work. But the next time you get a bad back, neither the anti-inflammatories or the painkillers work, but the osteopath fixes you! When you think about it, it's obvious – the solution will depend on what actually caused the backache. It could be a trapped nerve, muscle spasms, tendon problem, sciatica, misalignment, trapped vertebra, etc. None of the techniques you applied "don't work", but each is designed for a different cause. It's the same with anxiety. Over the years, you've probably found certain things have helped you with your anxiety, but on other occasions, they've let you down. You might have discarded them because they failed to work. There will be others that you've tried, but which have not worked at all. But in all likelihood, these techniques probably work for certain types of anxiety but not others. It's horses for courses.

There are a huge number of possible solutions to backache. Painkillers (of which there are many), anti-inflammatories (of which there are many), osteopathy, chiropractic, special chairs, reiki, yoga, massage, meditation, acupuncture, reflexology, special cushions and pillows, swimming, flotation tanks, special shoes, surgery, physiotherapy, memory foam mattresses and so on. What would be useful is if we could put them into categories, for example, muscle treatments, joint treatments, alignment treatments. Then if we can identify the cause of our backache, we can easily then go to the right category of treatments and pick out a solution that suits our particular situation.

This is exactly what we need to do with anxiety. We need to sort all the possible approaches to anxiety into categories, then identify the type of anxiety we have so we can choose the right category of solutions. We'll identify the different categories in Chapter 2. I'll look at each category in detail and introduce you to some staple techniques that belong to each one. At the end of that process, you'll have at least two techniques from each category in your anxiety-busting arsenal.

It's not all about worries

Having developed your arsenal, you'll then go on to learn to diagnose your own current anxiety and its causes, so you know which category(ies) are going to be effective in dealing with it. Of course, the physical fight-or-flight response is the same every time – the pupils dilate, the heart rate increases, etc. But there are many different things that may be triggering it, and the thoughts and feelings associated with it vary dramatically. *It's not all caused by what we think we are "worried" or "anxious" about.*

Obviously, the difference between us and an animal such as a wildebeest is that we are not literally roaming around in the wilds with natural predators to worry about. We are civilized and socialised, and our lives are much more complex. OK, so if a swarm of bees flies towards you, or you hear an explosion nearby, then your fight-or-flight mode is just like that of the animal – there is a real situation that demands an immediate, instinctual response. But our ability to think about the future is where the connection with "worrying" comes in. For example, you might have an important interview or exam tomorrow. You are worried. You might have just opened a letter and seen a huge electricity bill staring you in the face, and you don't have the money to pay for it. That certainly makes me worry. There are so many threats to our lives, and to our livelihoods. Some are about what is happening, or about to happen, or what might happen later on, or what could possibly happen at some point. These future possibilities are perceived as threats and so we go into fight-or-flight mode.

But there are other reasons it may be triggered. It could be due to changes in our hormone levels, or other chemicals in the brain, which in turn can be brought about by a number of things. It could be caused by our body dealing with allergies, addictions, illnesses or injuries. It can be triggered because we're excited about something (feeling "stoked" is exactly the same state of anxiety as when we feel "worried", we just perceive it differently). It can be triggered by being overworked or overloaded or being in a pressurised situation. It can be contagious, and if you are spending time around an anxious personality, this can trigger yours. It can be caused by relational problems, such as arguments, disappointment, rejection or frustrations with/from people around you.

As I said, worrying is just one of these possible causes, and I believe it's really important to make this distinction: *anxiety is not the same as worrying. There are many other causes of anxiety.* So, if we want to treat a bout of anxiety, it would be a big help if we can figure out what's causing it.

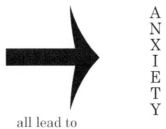

Reaction to threat in the here-and-now
Hormonal & chemical fluctuations
Other physical changes & conditions
Excitement
Worry
Overburdened/overload
Other pressurised situation
Addiction
Contagion
Relational problems
Aftermath of a worry

all lead to

ANXIETY

When we're anxious, that is, in fight-or-flight mode, we will often feel worried, but not always. We can be anxious without being worried. We can be anxious without even being aware that we're anxious! Does it matter if we're not aware? Well, yes, because it will be taking its toll on us physically and possibly affecting our behaviour without us knowing, making us irritable, angry or nervous, for example.

In Chapter 3, we'll look at this more closely. We'll explore how to tell if we're anxious, figure out why and immediately put into place some things to help manage it. We'll also talk about the times when we're not anxious, because they are important as well.

Different types of worry

Some of us are more prone to particular thought patterns that have been given names suggesting that they are types of anxiety: health anxiety, performance anxiety, social anxiety, just to name a few. If you think about it, these are all descriptions of patterns of worries associated with anxiety, rather than different *causes* of anxiety. Others have what the medical profession likes to call "generalized anxiety disorder" (or GAD for short). This is just their way of saying a person tends to worry about any number of different things at once. I don't think this label of "generalized anxiety disorder" is very useful, because when we worry about a few things, there's often just one single cause (not necessarily even a worry), and these other worries are actually like symptoms that have come along in a kind of cascade effect. It's like when your immune system is low, and you catch all sorts of bugs: you haven't got generalized bug disorder! Something has caused the system to be low in the first place. We need to identify what, otherwise we'll be chasing our tails trying to stop ourselves from worrying about each of the things that we're worrying about.

I'd like to ask you for now to forget about these distinctions – health anxiety[3], performance anxiety, phobias, GAD etc. For me, if we see anxiety as that fight-or-flight mode getting triggered too often, too fiercely, or for too long, then any solution has three elements. *We need to figure out how to relieve the symptoms of anxiety when they occur, to figure out why our fight-or-flight mode is triggered more than the average person, and we need to put in place measures to reduce or even prevent anxiety from occurring.* This is true whether the anxiety is caused by worrying, or hormones, or a reaction to something in our diet, or whatever.

But even when it really is a worry that's causing the anxiety, what works in some situations is totally inappropriate in another. For example, I might wake up one morning feeling so anxious I don't want to get out of bed. I don't really know why I'm worried about going to work, but I feel quite terrified about doing so. Or I might find myself constantly worrying that I don't have enough money, and it is causing a nagging, low-level but longer lasting anxiety. I would argue that *you need a very different approach to the first situation than the second.* When looking at worry-anxiety, there are four aspects to worrying that can vary: the degree of terror that you're feeling (I'm using the word "terror" here but you might not experience it as that – it might be experienced as panic, illness etc); how soon the feared event is going to happen; how likely it is to happen; and how severe or serious the feared thing is. The first two speak to the *urgency* of the worry, and the second two speak to the *appropriateness* of the worry.

---

[3] Having said that, I will pay some special attention to health anxiety at some points, because it is a particularly difficult form: worrying about health makes us anxious, the anxiety produces physical symptoms which make us feel worse, which we interpret as a further deterioration in our health, which makes us worry even more, and so on.

Looking at these four elements in terms of urgency and appropriateness will help you to select the right category of approach to managing your worry-anxiety. In Chapter 4, we'll identify each element, learn to identify the urgency and appropriateness of the worry and prescribe ourselves the right approach based on our findings.

Look at the appropriateness dimension. Recently one of my friends, let's call her Barbara, was anxious about having to have heart surgery a few weeks later. I'd say that was a case of highly appropriate anxiety – it was a very dangerous operation and there was a fair chance she could die. Meanwhile, another friend, let's call her Susan, was anxious that people at an event she was going to would see a wart on her arm even though she was going to wear long sleeves. This is less appropriate anxiety. You can imagine that what might help Barbara here might not help Susan, and vice versa. It's common sense, yet *anxiety is always just bundled up and treated as if it's one thing, when it's not.*

It also stands to reason that just because Barbara's situation was clearly more appropriate-to-be-anxious-about than Susan's, it doesn't mean that Susan's anxiety was less real, or less needed to be treated, or in fact that Susan's distress was any less than Barbara's. It was just a clearly different degree of appropriateness. In fact, Susan's event was the same day, and she was much more agitated than Barbara, so you could argue that the urgency was greater in Susan's case. So again, this more urgent, pressing need required a different approach – a different category of technique – to the less pressing need.

Suffice it to say at this stage that when it comes to addressing anxiety, it's horses for courses, and what I think is unique about this book is that it will help you target your anxiety correctly. Think of it this way: unless we diagnose our anxiety type better, we are not going to be able to treat it effectively, just as if your backache isn't diagnosed correctly, you're probably not going to get the right treatment.

Why am I an anxious person?

But why do we have Type 2 anxiety in the first place? What makes us more likely to be anxious than the next person, and what techniques and therapies can we use to reduce or manage that underlying proneness? In Chapter 5, we're going to drill down a bit into the causes of your proneness to being in fight-or-flight too often or for too long. Understanding this probably won't make it go away, but it will determine the best approach to dealing with it over the long run. We will try to establish the cause of your over-sensitive fight-or-flight triggering mechanism. It can be chemical, faulty thinking, physical, social, nutritional, situational, genetic, psychological (a phobia for example) or even habitual ... or a combination of some or all of these. We need to know which, and then we can start working on solutions that can help us manage, control and reduce this tendency in the long run.

Living with anxiety

The final element in treating anxiety is to find ways to stop it from happening in the first place and nip it in the bud when it starts. In Chapter 6, we'll develop good preventative practices so that anxiety doesn't creep up on us so easily and so we can manage it better when it does happen. This includes a special section that I encourage you to show to people close to you, who experience your anxiety on a regular basis. These are the members of your herd who would be happily grazing in the field until you send up the lion alert and call them to action. They probably get very frustrated by these false alarms. How they perceive your experience and how they react can have a big effect on you and really help you when you have a bout of anxiety.

I'm not promising a miracle cure in this book. *At the end of the day, you'll still have an oversensitive fight-or-flight response, just as I have still, and always will have.* I gave my wife a copy of the first draft of this book to read a few weeks ago and after a few days I asked her whether she'd read it. "It's really hard to read a book you've written on anxiety when you're busy having an anxiety meltdown in front of me over something you really don't need to be anxious about!" In other words, I'm not exactly the best advert for my own book. In my defence, I'd say we have to be realistic about our expectations. If we can reduce the number of times we have a bout of anxiety by say 70%, reduce the duration of a bout by 70%, and reduce the degree of terror by 70%, then life will be a lot easier!

Chapter 2: TECHNIQUES AND SOLUTIONS

In this chapter:
- We'll look at six completely different categories of techniques and approaches you can use to deal with anxiety
- You'll learn at least two techniques from each of the six categories
- You'll complete your technique inventory (or arsenal of weapons)

The different approaches to treating anxiety

We all know and have probably tried an awful lot of different techniques and treatments for dealing with anxiety. However, as I said above, this tends to be very hit-and-miss. I, for one, never really analysed what the aim of each solution really was. If we think of anxiety as being in fight-or-flight mode, then the goal of any solution should be to reduce the time spent in that mode. But how do we go about that? I would argue that any technique you might employ will belong to one of the following categories:

Calming Techniques

These are techniques that aim to help you to find your centre and feel calmer. They are by nature quite immediate, and obviously more suited to situations when you are highly agitated, upset, afraid and/or panicky.

Physical Techniques

These are interventions that involve body movement. They are not all purely physical, and some have a very spiritual component (e.g. yoga) but they are in this category because there are particular anxiety types that respond very well to a physical approach.

Strengthening Techniques

These are techniques that aim to soothe and strengthen your mind, your focus, and your spirit, and to put you more in charge of your worrying thoughts.

Philosophical Techniques

These techniques are targeted at worry-anxiety that is based on something inevitable that is hard to come to terms with. They look to make sense of tragedy, death, loss and isolation by finding meaning and reflecting on what it is to be human.

Practical Techniques

This category includes exercises and techniques that work at a practical level, whether to distract you from your anxiety, to help you focus on other things, and so on.

Medical Techniques

Fight-or-flight can be altered chemically, using conventional western and alternative medicines.

It stands to reason that each of these categories might be more or less useful in different anxiety situations. So it would be very useful if you knew a couple of techniques from each category, so you can adapt your approach depending on the situation at hand. So in the following sections, we'll look at each of these 6 categories in turn and I'll present a range of techniques for you to choose from. By the end of Chapter 2, you will have learned 12 techniques - two techniques from each category – and in so doing you'll have given yourself all the equipment you need to treat different types of anxiety. You'll then be armed and ready to go on with the rest of the book, where you'll learn how to diagnose your current anxiety, what the reasons are for your predisposition to anxiety, and how to prevent and manage anxiety on an ongoing basis.

Calming Techniques

The basic principle of calming techniques is to tell your brain that everything is OK and that it's safe to come out of fight-or-flight mode. This can be done physically, by altering our breathing, posture etc, or cognitively, by sending thoughts to the fight-or-flight governor in our brain, or a combination of the two. You should learn at least two calming techniques. In this section, I'll introduce you to three: simple breathing exercises, music and autogenic training. You'll find a number of others in Appendix A. You can learn these as well as, or instead of, the three I'm going to talk about here – have a browse in Appendix A and go with whichever work(s) best for you.

Breathing Exercises

You may have tried breathing exercises before and thought it was all a bit pointless and irritating. I think it's about expectations. Breathing exercises are not going to fix your anxiety, but they will help. It may only be 5 or 10%, but they will help. It's a very good place to start, especially when your degree of terror is high. It costs nothing to learn, it takes very little time to perform and you can do it absolutely anywhere. It is usually without side effects, but if done incorrectly there is a slight chance you might hyperventilate, so be sure to learn a proper technique. There are different types of breathing exercise, it's not just all about deep breathing. Find one that seems to work best for you. Add this to your arsenal right now by doing the exercise on the next page.

Alternatively, look at some of the different techniques on different websites, such as
http://healthland.time.com/2012/10/08/6-breathing-exercises-to-relax-in-10-minutes-or-less/
https://draxe.com/breathing-exercises/
https://www.nhs.uk/conditions/stress-anxiety-depression/ways-relieve-stress/

Try a few and pick one or more that you feel suit(s) you best. Go over the exercise a few times until you have it committed to memory, so that from now on, you always have it available for times of high anxiety.

1. *Sit or lie in a relaxed position.*
2. *Put your right hand on your chest and the left on your stomach.*
3. *Close your mouth and breathe in slowly through your nose, counting to ten, continuing to inhale as you feel your stomach filling under your left hand. As you become experienced, you can also start to fill your chest after filling your stomach (allowing the right hand to be raised by the inhaled air after the left is already raised).*
4. *Hold your breath for a few seconds (maybe three, four or five, as is comfortable)*
5. *Purse your lips and breathe out, forcing the air through your pursed lips like air coming out of a tyre. Continue, counting to ten, until all the air has been exhaled.*
6. *Hold your breath for a few seconds (three, four or five, as is comfortable)*
7. *Repeat 1-6 for a minimum of ten times and a maximum of thirty times.*

Don't try to push yourself or go harder. Don't breathe in through your mouth or gulp the air. If at any point you feel light headed, breathe too fast or feel more, rather than less anxious, just stop the exercise and breathe normally.

Music

You may or may not be surprised to know that music has an incredibly good record in scientific studies[4] in terms of helping anxiety. It is increasingly used by the medical profession around the world. *Research strongly suggests that it can reduce anxiety by an average of 30%*, which is pretty impressive. Studies have even gone so far as to recommend that the music should be non-lyrical and between 60-80 beats per minute, but my instincts tell me that sounds a little too prescriptive! Before you go rushing off for your iPod, though, think about the circumstances in which you'll be listening to the music. Much of the research has compared, for example, patients in hospital listening to music vs. those who aren't, but these are people who are generally in a *high immediacy worry type* situation. In other situations, and especially for the chronic anxiety sufferer, sitting quietly listening to music to try to calm yourself might even make you more

---

[4] See for example https://www.researchgate.net/publication/5457754_The_Anxiety-_and_Pain-Reducing_Effects_of_Music_Interventions_A_Systematic_Review

anxious, because you might end up sitting thinking anxious thoughts when the best approach is to distract yourself or do something more physical (both of which I'll talk about below). But certainly, in situations of high immediacy and likelihood, music can be a very powerful tool.

It might be a good idea, when you are not so stressed and have some time, to make yourself a playlist (or, if you're old school, a compilation tape or CD) of music you find most relaxing, and keep it handy to play when you're next in an anxiety-provoking situation. I would also suggest that you seek out stuff that would not be your usual style. In the period of my life when my anxiety was at its worst, I found that classical music worked the best for me (I remember having a CD called "Smooth Classics for Rough Days") in terms of calming me and bringing me out of fight-or-flight. But classical music is not something I normally listen to the rest of the time.

Exercise 2 **Calming Playlist**

Make a playlist or other form of compilation of calming music that you can play when you have anxiety.

Another way of using music to combat anxiety that works for some people is to do the exact opposite of the calming approach. Play extremely emotional, energetic, loud music, sing out loud to it at the top of your voice, feel the emotion and release all that tension you're your body (Dance therapy is also valuable in this way). Rather than trying to turn off fight-or-flight here, you're actually burning it up, using it up and wearing it out. (This really belongs in the next category of techniques – Physical).

Autogenic Training

Autogenic Training (AT), also sometimes called *autogenic therapy*, is a technique specifically designed to take us out of fight-or-flight mode using a form of self-hypnosis focusing on body awareness. It is relatively little known but is beginning to gain a fan base and some very respectable results in scientific research[5]. I personally find it particularly useful when I'm struggling to get to sleep due to my busy head. It is easy to learn, being basically a series of self-statements that you go through that focus on

---

[5] See, for example,
https://pdfs.semanticscholar.org/b7fb/893ec9562db3950944af21209e153660b2e3.pdf

different areas of your body. The process of repeating the body awareness statements puts you in a relaxed state (what hypnotists might call, a state of suggestibility), and once in this state, you can then repeat a short phrase of your choosing – a "resolution", around 30 times, which helps you to calm down and return from fight-or-flight to a normal state. This could be something like:

I am strong and powerful, safe and protected
Or
I am calm and brave, relaxed and confident
Or, if your aim is to sleep
I am calm and sleepy

On the next page you'll see the basic routine[6] that you perform before repeating your resolution. Note that there are slightly different versions of the script available at these sites:
http://welz.us/Autogenic.pdf (a traditional paper introducing the technique, written in 1991)
http://www.syncsouls.de/audiobook-autogenic-training-1.asp (this site also has good Youtube videos and audio downloads).

I will talk more about self-hypnosis in broader terms, in the *Strengthening* section, below. But in terms of using autogenics for relaxation, it can be extremely effective and can very quickly bring you out of, or reduce, flight-or-flight.

Try to learn the script off by heart, so you can apply it whenever you need a calming technique.

---

[6] I adapted this from
http://www.balloontothemoon.com/AutogenicTrainingSampleScript.pdf)

Exercise 3 **Autogenic training**

Get into a comfortable position, take a deep breath and close your eyes.
Repeat each phrase quietly in your mind—slowly and
rhythmically. Let's begin...

I am calm and relaxed.
My right arm is heavy. (Repeat 3 times).
My left arm is heavy. (Repeat 3 times).
My arms are heavy. (Repeat 3 times).

I am calm and relaxed.
My right leg is heavy. (Repeat 3 times).
My left leg is heavy. (Repeat 3 times).
My legs are heavy. (Repeat 3 times).

I am calm and relaxed.
My right hand is warm. (Repeat 3 times).
My left hand is warm. (Repeat 3 times).
My hands are warm. (Repeat 3 times).

I am calm and relaxed.
My right foot is warm. (Repeat 3 times).
My left foot is warm. (Repeat 3 times).
My feet are warm. (Repeat 3 times).

I am calm and relaxed.
My heartbeat is calm and regular. (Repeat 3 times). My breathing is calm
and regular. (Repeat 3 times). My solar plexus is warm. (Repeat 3 times).
My forehead is cool. (Repeat 3 times).

I am very calm and relaxed.

Now follow this by repeating your resolution thirty times.

Physical Techniques

Exercise of Any Sort

If you're like me, you might be naturally suspicious of being recommended or prescribed exercise for anxiety, because it seems to be prescribed for everything, and the very idea of it can be stressful. This is because being in fight-or-flight all the time is exhausting, so with anxiety comes a great deal of tiredness and a real lack of energy. The last thing you want to hear is to take exercise. However, whether we like it or not, *studies have shown really conclusively that exercise helps with anxiety,* and at the opposite end of the spectrum, that *there is a very strong correlation between a lack of physical activity and the development of anxiety*[7].

One explanation for this is that sometimes anxiety can be an expression of unused energy. The human body is meant to be mobile, but modern life often has us sitting in one place for a big part of our day, and that lack of movement creates physical tension. The chemicals involved in the fight-or-flight system – particularly cortisol, is used up by exercise, and so it tends to take you out of fight-or-flight. This is the natural order of things, so when you are too still, these chemicals will not be being used in the right way and the body will be in fight-or-flight when it doesn't need to be. Also, too much cortisol can interfere with your sleep patterns, adding to your anxiety and your tiredness in a vicious circle.

At the same time that exercise reduces cortisol, the chemical that fight-or-flight feeds off, it also produces other chemicals called endorphins, which make you feel happy (and also reduce pain), in other words, chemicals that will thwart your anxious thoughts. Add to that the fact that it is actually good for you generally, will make you fitter, stronger, more confident, it will keep your muscles and your body chemistry working well and will help you to think more clearly – and even feel better about yourself generally. I would say *if you had to choose just one thing out of all the techniques discussed in this book, exercise is the most important.*

Unless you're already a fit and sporty type of person, don't go rushing out and join a gym. Start gently and work your way up. Or don't even work your way up – even gentle exercise for 20 minutes or so a day may be all you need to get the maximum benefit for your anxiety. In fact, there's probably a peak level of exercise, and I would argue that if you go too over-the-top with

---

[7] See for example
https://bmcpublichealth.biomedcentral.com/articles/10.1186/s12889-015-1843-x

exercise, it might start to increase anxiety again. It might put a strain on your body, causing injuries and wear and tear that start to make life difficult. Also, that endorphin rush that you get from exercise can be very addictive and so you can get withdrawal anxiety when you can't exercise for whatever reason.

The hardest part is starting to do this. Try to choose something that you will enjoy, that will be easy to fit into your daily routine and that isn't too strenuous or difficult to begin with. Likewise, if you're used to doing exercise already but are struggling with anxiety, lower the intensity level. If your level is normally quite intense, go for moderate, and if your normal level is moderate, go for gentle exercise.

> *Exercise 4* **Couch exercises**
>
> *This is a great idea for people who don't get enough regular exercise.*
> *Most of us have a regular point in the day when we are sitting at home on our sofa. Set that time every day (say perhaps when watching your favourite soap, or the news) and set a 10-minute timer. Without getting up off the sofa, perform some gentle physical exercises for those 10 minutes every day.*
>
> *Use routines you find on Youtube, such as*
> *https://www.youtube.com/watch?v=Q5C2V5ovZvk.*
>
> *Get family members to help you stick to it!*

In terms of physical exercise, it doesn't matter what you do, but it's important that you do something. Don't do too much, and don't beat yourself up when you don't always manage to do it.

Yoga

As it is a holistic, mind-body practice, I could put yoga into any of these categories – calming, physical, strengthening, philosophical and practical. I've chosen to put it here in the physical section because even if you don't get completely into the whole spiritual side of yoga, its exercises - the physical stretches and poses - are extremely beneficial to anxiety on their own. They incorporate breathing exercises such as those I discussed above in the "calming" techniques above, but they also stretch and strengthen tense muscles throughout the body that are both a result of anxiety, and a cause of it.

Yoga is one of those things that you might not realise is helping, and people (myself included) often fall out of the habit when things are going well, and anxiety is low. Then before we know it, we are feeling anxious again and have to pick the yoga back up, dust it off and get it working for us again!

There are many different forms of yoga, some are more physically demanding than others. If you are trying yoga for the first time, Google™ the different forms and try to find one that sounds right for you.[8] Before you go rushing off to join a class, I would recommend you then find a beginner's class on YouTube, try it and see how it feels.

Whilst yoga should be the perfect antidote to anxiety, I have known people who have found that the dedication they felt it required put too much of a time demand on their week, and so it became a cause of stress. We don't want that. But don't throw the baby out with the bathwater. As I said, *even just doing 15 – 20 minutes, 3 or 4 times a week will have a really good effect on your anxiety levels.* I try to do a very gentle 15-minute session every day. I have to push myself to do it every time. If I have a very physical day, I'll not make myself do it, and I'll also give myself permission to miss a day here and there, so in the end I probably only do it 2 or 3 times a week. But that is enough to feel some benefit. Forcing yourself to do something is stressful, so find the balance between when to push yourself and when to give yourself a break.

If you really get into the whole yoga way of life, it will literally mean a change of life style, but will include spiritual elements, meditation, mindfulness and so many other wonderfully anxiety-ridding things. Although I can see the benefits so clearly, I've never been able to commit to something so all-encompassing. I'm not even sure I want "inner peace" because I want to feel adrenaline and a buzz and a rush (I am recognising that actually, I don't want to be completely without anxiety!) But if you can and want to, do it. If it's right for you, it will almost certainly will be a huge help with your anxiety, particularly for non-immediate types.

Play

When we are worried, our worries are nearly always about adult things – work, health, money, etc. Serious stuff. If you accept the idea that we all have an "inner child", then he or she probably gets pretty neglected when

---

[8] There is a good introduction at https://www.gaiam.com/blogs/discover/a-beginners-guide-to-8-major-styles-of-yoga.

the adult part of us is preoccupied with all these worries. And just like a real child, if we don't give our inner child enough attention, she will probably "play up" – tantrums, tears, or rebellion – or she'll withdraw. She will be scared. These feelings and this behaviour become part of our anxiety and make us feel worse about ourselves. This is where play comes in. If your anxiety will allow you to take some time out in your day, preferably, every day – to just get in touch with your inner child and play, you will find some benefit. Anything that's fun and is playing will work, but best of all would be games with a physical element to them, because you are then combining play with exercise (so for example, kicking a ball about may be more anxiety-reducing than, say playing a computer game). But the whole point of play is that it's fun and it's a choice, so don't make yourself play a certain way, or for a certain length of time. Just play!

---

*Exercise 5 **The Toy Shop***

Go to a toy shop and buy something for your inner child to play or do. It should be something you can enjoy, play regularly and that is practical. It can be anything you like – Lego, skateboard, playdough, roller skates, ice skates, hoverboard, drone, board game, skipping rope, train set ... whatever your inner child wants!

There are many other physically based techniques that can help with anxiety. I've suggested some in Appendix A.

Strengthening Techniques

One of the worst aspects of anxiety is fear. Those of us who are long-term anxiety sufferers develop a fearful mindset that becomes very engrained and is difficult to shift. Think of your thoughts as streams of water flowing downhill. Over time, grooves are formed and so the water will always tend to follow that same groove. When anxiety is triggered, your thinking might always follow that same, fearful, negative or pessimistic groove. What we need to do is get our spades out and dig ourselves a new channel for our thoughts to follow – one that's more productive, positive and optimistic. If you were to have cognitive behavioural therapy or something similar, you would be challenged to think in different ways – to try to retrain your brain to naturally follow a different path.

Another aspect of anxiety is what I would call *dread*. It's that feeling of absolute horror that seems to take over your whole body and fill you with terror. For people with Type 1 anxiety, this dread is reserved for genuine life-or-death situations, but those of us with Type 2 can feel that dread over things that are really not that bad. *We know in our heads that the dread is inappropriate, but that doesn't help, because, again, we are back to the fact that it's an involuntary response.*

A positive mindset does not help you to avoid anxiety, but it helps you through it. If, say, 50% of the symptoms of your anxiety is that horrible fear, that sense of being unable to cope, that feeling of being powerless and small, then the ability to tackle the situation with a strong mindset will remove a major chunk of the problem. Whist having cognitive therapy is perhaps the Rolls Royce way of developing a more positive mindset, there are many techniques you can follow to strengthen your resolve that you can teach yourself.

Visualisations – Developing your Inner Demon and Inner Hero

This is a technique I use all the time and it is a tremendous help to me and to people I've taught to use it. It can take any form you want and is limited only by your imagination – you can see it as a kind of focussed daydream that you use to help you feel a certain way.

When we are anxious, the anxious thoughts fill our head. If you see it as a voice inside your head, it is the loudest one, and drowns out all the others. The "I'm going to forget my lines now", or "It's cancer, I'm really sick", or the "I can't go in, I can't face those people" messages are so loud that we feel they are the only messages, that they define or own us.

What we have to do is see that it is just one message, or voice, inside our head, and create room for other voices.

Do the exercise on the following page. If you can get into this way of thinking, you will be able to develop that strong voice more and more, and whilst you can't (and mustn't) kill off your anxiety voice, he will no longer be able to run riot around your head and take over the entire show.

This may all sound very strange, but with enough imagination and a little persistence, you can summon up this sort of mental imagery to help you reduce your anxiety and embolden you when dealing with a difficult situation.

If you see your anxiety as a powerful, fearful thing rather than a wimpy character, type, imagine a different type of character, such as an "evil" anxiety lord that has to be defeated. It's totally up to you as to what kind of personality you give your anxiety, as long as his messages, or dialogue, represents your anxiety. You may have more than one character if you have different types of anxiety at any particular time and you may have more than one character who puts them in their place.

I would really like one of the things you take from this book to be an inner hero, captain or general, who you can summon up in your mind to put your fearful or negative thoughts to one side and replace them with "we're going to do this and nothing's going to stop us" thoughts. But if it really isn't for you, then please at least take one thing from this section: the idea that *your anxiety is not the whole of you and does not define you. Name it, identify those thoughts as just one particular strain of thoughts, and try to develop counteracting thoughts.*

The Anxiety Coach

When our own strength is not enough on its own, or we just want some extra support, it would be really helpful if we could have someone in our corner that can encourage us through. Often, we are a bit ashamed or embarrassed about our anxiety and this can stop us from asking for help from those around us. But in the right hands, that kind of help can be absolutely invaluable, and one of our best weapons against anxiety. In my experience, the problem is not usually that there's nobody willing to help, but rather, that our loved ones don't really know what to do or say for the best. They will tend to either try to reassure us and tell us the feared thing won't happen, or they'll try to explain to us why our anxiety is illogical, excessive or unreasonable, which is unhelpful, because we know that don't we? And knowing it doesn't help. Worse, you feel stupid and you can feel like you're letting them down. My solution is simple. Let's train them to be a better support! If we can give them instructions, then we could have a really effective coach in our corner.

If there's someone who you would like to ask and who would like to give it a try, do the exercise on the next page. If you're lucky and you find someone who can do this as and when you need it, I would suggest that you periodically give them the instructions again (tell them it's what the book tells you to do). Otherwise, most people will tend to forget some of the key elements of these instructions and think it's just their own magnificence that's helping you, rather than the fact that they're doing the things you need!

Having the right support is invaluable in dealing with anxiety. I've included a whole section in Chapter 6, Helping those Around you to Understand and Manage your Anxiety, for people close to you to read. This may also help to supplement the anxiety coach training we're doing here.

Ask someone sensitive who you trust if they would be willing to be your anxiety coach. If you want to try it just once, explain to them that there's a situation you're facing that is causing you anxiety and that you would like them in your corner. Otherwise, simply tell them that you have issues with anxiety and would like to call on them now and again. If they say yes, give them the following note:

Thank you for being my anxiety coach...

... I am going to be feeling very anxious while facing the following situation: [state the feared situation in as few words as possible, maybe 20 words or so]. OR... I have ongoing issues with anxiety ...

... and I would like to be able to contact you, or for you to be with me, when I need extra strength. Please do the following:

- *Let me talk about my fears, just listening and accepting and not trying to fix things.*
- *Remind me I can do this*
- *Motivate me; ask me to tell you why getting through this is important*
- *Remind me, or ask me to tell you, about other difficult situations that I've faced and survived*
- *Ask me what my strengths are and why they'll help me get through this*
- *Remind me that you're there for me no matter what and we'll get through it together*
- *If you're there with me, offer to hold my hand and/or give me a hug.*

Please don't do the following:

- *Get into a debate about my worries*
- *Talk about your own worries or compare mine to yours, or me to you, unless I specifically ask you to*
- *Try to reason with me or persuade me to think differently*
- *Reassure me and tell me everything's going to be OK, unless I ask you to*
- *Get frustrated or impatient with me. I might not be easy to listen to!*

Self-Hypnosis

For many of us, the word "hypnosis" conjures up images of stage hypnotists making people believe they're farmyard animals, but in reality, it isn't anything to fear and mostly it is about being in a completely relaxed state. It is a trance-like state where we're switched off to the world around us. When we are in such a state, we are more "suggestible" (open to suggestions), and these suggestions can come from ourselves, not just other people. So, self-hypnosis can be a very effective tool.

Before you start, think about what you want to achieve. Try to pick two emotions that you'd like to feel instead of anxious. Use words such as cool, relaxed, calm, confident, strong, serene, bold, brave. Once you have your key words, you are ready to start the self-hypnosis. You're going to put yourself in that trance-like state, then tell yourself "I am calm and brave", for example.

In terms of the actual technique you use to put you into your suggestible state, there are various methods, and you should choose one that suits you. For example, one might ask you to imagine walking down stairs into water, but if you have a fear of drowning, this wouldn't work for you!

Exercise 8 **Self-hypnosis**

One self-hypnosis method is to visualise a peaceful scene that you explore until you find a figure representing yourself, then when you do so, tell your figure-self the key words. Start by sitting somewhere quiet and warm (not hot). Close your eyes and start counting backwards from 100. Place yourself at the start of the scene and start to walk around. As you count reaches about 90, can you see your figure-self in the distance? Go toward yourself, still counting backward. As your count reaches 75, take your time and look at the scene around you, it is peaceful and comforting. As your count reaches 50, you start to get closer to your figure-self. When you're ready, you reach the figure of yourself, and take your own hand. Look into your figure self's eyes and say your key phrase. "I am calm and brave". Make sure your figure-self hears it, then smile and slowly turn away. When you're ready, walk slowly back to the starting point, where you'll exit the hypnosis. Take a few seconds before opening your eyes and coming out of your trance.

Now, when you are next in an anxiety-provoking situation, say "I am calm and brave", out loud, or under your breath, or even just in your head. You will find that alongside your anxiety, you start to feel those strengthening emotions immediately.

There's another method at https://hypnosistrainingacademy.com/self-hypnosis-how-to-hypnotize-yourself/ and plenty more, if my suggested one doesn't work for you.

Sounds too easy? Well, *self-hypnosis really is much simpler than you would think*. You might need to try the visualisation a few times before it really has an effect, but you might not. It won't transform you into a superhero, it is subtler than you would imagine, but it might give you, say 20%-30% more confidence when facing your anxiety, which will be a big help.

Appendix A contains a number of other strengthening techniques. You should learn at least two strengthening techniques and have them in your arsenal to help you through anxious episodes.

Philosophical Techniques

Sometimes anxiety is based on a very deep and real fear about something that's very likely to happen, or even unavoidable. In these cases, looking deeper into the meaning of life, why we are here and what it's all about, might offer a fresh way to "frame" your concerns and make sense of your anxiety. Challenging our anxious thoughts and reminding ourselves of the bigger picture is important. Anxiety is part of what it is to be human and has a relationship with beliefs, religion, spirituality and existence, so addressing the philosophical dimension can speak directly to the source of the problem, especially in worry-based anxiety.

Living for Today

Worrying is based in the future – it's about what might happen. In fact, anxiety is by its very nature set in the future: the fight-or-flight response is *preparing* us for action, rather than actually *taking* action in the here-and-now. We live our lives worrying about tomorrow rather than actually being present in the here-and-now.

Being in the absolute here-and-now involves focussing on what is going on around us, on our sensations and senses. Mindfulness is an excellent technique for bringing yourself into the present. However, in terms of a philosophical approach to anxiety, it's not always necessary to aim for that absolute state of being in the moment. How about focussing on the next hour, or the next day? What if this was my last day on earth? Would I spend it worrying about stuff? No. So why not make today a special day, and worry about tomorrow when it comes? Doing so will take you out of fight-or-flight and replace it with something pleasant. In this practical exercise, I want you to think about how you can get the most out of today, and I want this to become an exercise you repeat as often as you possibly can.

Exercise 9 **Living for Today**

Try to plan out your day so you can squeeze the best out of it, no matter what your situation. Tell yourself "today is going to be a good day". Or just focus on the next hour. How can I make the next day or hour special? Meaningful? Fun? Happy? Productive? Can you treat yourself to something lovely? Can you carve out a special moment with someone you care about? What would be fun or meaningful, what could make you laugh or smile or feel love today? Don't focus on anything to do with planning even a couple of days into the future. Focus on anything to do with today and make today count. You might want to set reminders, or an alarm clock, a couple of times during the day so you can make sure you're following through with the plan.

Turning Outward/Helping Others

This is a very simple approach to anxiety that can yield surprisingly powerful and immediate results. In addition to being future-based, *anxiety is also by its very nature an acute, often obsessive "looking inward" at one's self,* what I am doing, what I am feeling, what is going on inside my head, what is going on inside my body. It's not that the trigger is something within the self (let's say, it's an important speech that you have to give tomorrow), but the focus of most of your thoughts as a result of that trigger is about yourself (e.g. What if I fail? What if I forget my words? What if people laugh at me? What if I stutter?) Even if we're worrying about someone else, we are still turned inward (e.g. What if my friend goes to prison? How am I going to help her and her family? What do I say to her? Who am I going to talk to? Am I strong enough to go to visit her? etc.)

Some time ago I noticed that my anxiety seemed to disappear when I was actually in session with my therapy clients. I realised that there is no need for me to make a conscious effort to leave my own worries at the door when I go into a therapy session, it is just a very natural thing that happens when I focus on another person. I figured out that the reason for this absence of anxiety was that I was focusing outward, on other people, rather than inward and on myself. Relief from my own worries is therefore a by-product of providing therapy for other people (perhaps I should pay my clients for the time, rather than the other way around!) *This focussing outward is tremendously powerful* in terms of dealing with my own worry-anxiety, and I've learned to use it not just in therapy, but in general, as a tool to push myself out of fight-or-flight.

Exercise 10 **Turning outward**

If you're feeling very anxious about something, think of someone (or more than one person), and think of something you could do to make their day, week, or even life, better. If you're very short of time, it could be something as simple as sending them a message saying you miss them or love them. It could be picking up the phone and just asking them how they are and what is going on with their life. If possible, you could do them a favour you know would help them or meet up with them and take them out for dinner. Promote their business for them. Ideally it should be something that absorbs your attention for a reasonable amount of time, but if that's not possible, even something simple like commenting on some of their Facebook posts might do.

I am confident that you will find that for that time you have spent thinking of that other person, your anxiety will have reduced, at least a little. And you may also have the pleasing sensation of having done something good and making the world a better place.

Explore philosophy and existentialism

Looking deeper into the meaning of life, why we are here and what it's all about, might offer a fresh new challenge to your anxiety. Unfortunately, the world of philosophy is about as high-brow as it comes, so it's off-putting for a lot of people, which is a shame. The fact is, a lot of it isn't complicated at all – it's just written and taught in a really complicated way. Philosophy has been made so complicated that if you Google "main branches of philosophy", you'll see that there are four main branches ... no five ... no, six ... no, seven! Nobody seems to even be able to agree on basics such as these. But most agree that something called "metaphysics" is one of the main branches, and it's probably within metaphysics that you will find ideas that concern the meaning of life.

There are some good books that make philosophy more approachable, so if you can find such a book, or if you're academically gifted and aren't daunted by reading high-brow stuff, then just try reading about metaphysics for a week, to see if it grabs you or gives you anything to get you thinking differently.

A particular strand of philosophy that has helped me and others immensely in terms of anxiety is existentialism. In fact, existentialism gave rise to a whole branch of psychotherapy called existential psychotherapy, which I'll talk about below. But for the purposes of this section, existentialist philosophy is one that explores individual existence and what it means to be human. Some of the world's most famous philosophers were existentialists, for example, Kierkegaard, Jean Paul Sartre, Nietzsche, Camus, Dostoyevsky, William James, Heidegger, Simone de Beauvoir and Franz Kafka, to name but a few. It is all very dark and deep, at times morbid and depressing, so why am I recommending it as something that can help with anxiety? Well, because it addresses your anxiety in both accepting and challenging ways. For one thing, it starts with the assumption that *it's normal to be anxious, it is actually more normal than being non-anxious.* Please read Existential Therapy in Appendix B for a brief introduction on why it can be very helpful for anxiety. If that sounds like something you might want to try, find some introductory papers and books online and dip your toe in the water. Or, if you've already read or studied existential works, go back to them again.

Your belief system should also be a big help when it comes to dealing with anxiety, see More Philosophical Techniques in Appendix A for more on that. The important thing by the end of this section is that you have at least two philosophical techniques in your arsenal.

Practical Techniques

This category of techniques contains ideas for managing your anxiety in common sense, practical ways. I'm going to talk about four techniques that have very widespread applications, so they are particularly useful to add to your arsenal of weapons. However, they can be supplemented or replaced by any of those in Appendix A if they are more suited to your personal pattern of anxiety. The important thing at the end of this section is that you have learned at least two practical techniques.

Choose Fight or Flight

This technique is based on doing what the fight-or-flight mechanism was designed for. Look at the thing that's causing you anxiety. With some (but not all) worries, you have that very choice: you can try to avoid it (*flight*), or you can face up to it/go through it (*fight*). Sometimes it's best to do one and sometimes the other. Avoiding avoidable stressful situations (*flight*) is being kind to yourself, giving yourself a break. You'll be surprised how often you can do this, if you only give yourself permission. If it's a case of "I don't want to let anyone down", think about how you're letting yourself down by putting yourself through more stress that you don't have to. Give yourself a pass today. *It's OK!* On the other hand, confronting stressful situations (*fight*) takes away their power, and gives you confidence. Do you think you can tackle that thing today? Give yourself a little push. You'll feel a great sense of accomplishment.

Try to find a good balance between fight and flight. Pick your battles. Try to choose *fight* when the benefits to going through with something *for yourself* (not to people please) are worth fighting for. Try to choose *flight* when it's a lot of stress for something that's not that important, or when you just need to take a break from your anxiety.

Exercise 11 **Picking your battles.**

Do this exercise at a time when you are worried about more than one thing that you are supposed to do, or when you've got anxiety because of overload. Think about two of these worries. Choose one that you are going to avoid (flight), and one that you are going to confront (fight). For example, make an excuse and cancel going to that party you are worried about, but choose to make that phone call to book that medical test you've been avoiding.

Using fight-or-flight in this way can be very useful for getting rid of worries, because whether you choose fight or flight, it's no longer a worry, because it's dealt with. It sounds simple, and it is simple, but it's amazing how multiple worries just get piled up and we are like rabbits caught in the headlights and leave them on the worry pile.

Acceptance

The fight-or-flight technique can be good when we're worried about something that we're going to do, that we could choose not to do. But often we are worried about things that might happen to us, over which we have no control. And when we have anxiety, we don't like it, so it's natural to try to get rid of it. Unfortunately, these efforts to get rid of it, stop worrying, forget about it or push it away are usually disorganised and for many of us, it just leads to more worrying. *We become worried about the anxiety, and that just increases the anxiety. We feel it increasing and that makes us worry about it even more. I suggest that in many cases, up to 90% of our anxiety can be caused by this "metaphobic anxiety", or worrying about, focussing on, and reacting to the anxiety we have.* This is especially true for health anxiety, because we focus on the physical symptoms of anxiety, worry that they are the sign of something more dangerous or life threatening, and this worrying increases the anxiety and worsens the symptoms.

Anxiety's vicious circle

Clearly, there is one very important thing you must do. Try to accept that you are anxious today. You may even be very anxious, but it's OK. It's not going to kill you. You're not going to be stuck in it for the rest of your life, or even for the rest of this week. *Don't get anxious about being anxious. It will pass.* That is not to say we can't reduce or remove it, that's what this book is about. But let's try to do that in a dispassionate way, like we're taking out the rubbish, rather than panic about it and waste a lot of energy obsessing about it.

In accepting your anxiety today, you are taking away the worry you would have had about being anxious, which should reduce it quite a bit.

The Worry Hour

One of the debilitating aspects of worry-anxiety is that it pervades your day, you're distracted from life because you are obsessively worrying about whatever it is that's bothering you. It is overwhelming. But sometimes you can't just not worry about it and bury your head in the sand. Worriers tend also to be planners, and part of what you do when worrying is useful, in that you're anticipating something (or a number of things) happening and planning what you might do if it (they) happen(s). You are preparing yourself for an eventuality, so you can deal with it better when or if it happens, and that's a good thing. But it's not a good thing if that planning is circular and constant and is whirring around your head like a whirling dervish!

Let's take the two worries that are buzzing around in my head today. One is about the cold I have. As a health anxiety sufferer, I've been worrying that the cold is really something more serious and potentially terminal. The other issue was triggered by having to pay some bills and look at my financial situation, which started me worrying that I am going to run out of money and become poor. If I'm not careful and before I know it, these two thoughts might be constantly demanding my attention and keeping me in fight-or-flight. So I need to get them out of my head. On the other hand, it's no good simply telling myself not to worry about them, because there is a small chance that ignoring the concerns might be ignoring vital warning signs of a danger in my life. So, what should I do? Well, one thing I can do is to put them on a list and allocate an hour in the day in which I will spend worrying about the things on the list. During that hour, I might assess my cold, review how I'm treating it and decide whether at this stage to make an appointment to see the doctor. I might look at my finances and do some planning to try to make things better, consolidate my loans, etc. If I find myself thinking about my worries outside of the worry hour, I remind myself that now is not the time, and that the concerns will be addressed later.

The worry hour technique obviously does not work if the thing you're worried about is about to happen any second. But if your concerns are not so immediate, with a little practice it can give you the best of both worlds – *you still get a chance to do your worrying, but it doesn't take over your whole day and keep you in fight-or-flight the rest of the time.* You will find that because you're only addressing your concerns for an hour, your thinking about them will be more constructive, sharper and more productive. I also sometimes find that I get to the worry hour and don't want to do it, so I say to myself, I don't need to worry about these things today, I'll skip today's worry hour and worry about them tomorrow. Before you know it, you can go a whole day being virtually anxiety-free!

I really recommend the worry hour technique for habitual worriers.

The Three-week Rule

This is a technique that's particularly useful for people who suffer from health anxiety, although it can be used for a lot of other types of worry as well. A common pattern in health anxiety is that we become aware of a symptom, something different occurring on or inside our body, and become overly concerned about it, focus on it and imagine the worst. Some people start Googling™ the symptoms and inevitably end up staring at the part of the page where it says "in rare cases it might be a symptom of cancer/heart disease ..." or whatever. The "what if?" drives us into *high terror* anxiety. When people tell us "You're all right, it's just X", we can't accept it, because what if they're wrong? If this goes untreated because I'm ignoring it, it might be too late to treat when I finally go and get diagnosed!

Of course, the physical symptoms of anxiety then start to emerge, making the picture seem even worse – and these can include just about anything. We panic more because of these worsening symptoms, which makes us even worse, and this vicious circle can be terrifying, painful and exhausting (see also Acceptance). Here's the thing: STOP and do the following exercise.

Make a note of the date three weeks from today. Put a big X in your diary. If the symptoms have not improved by that date, you will go to the doctor. Three weeks is usually long enough for minor health issues to resolve themselves, and yet it is not so long a delay in seeking treatment that it would make the difference between life and death. In the meantime, treat it as if it's anxiety, even if you don't believe it is, using a combination of calming and physical methods as described above.

This three-week rule works at several levels. First, *it takes away the "should I, shouldn't I" stress about seeking treatment*, for now, which can make your load immediately lighter. It also works a bit like the worry hour, in that by scheduling the time when you will worry, it *allows you to focus on other things in the here-and-now*, giving you a break from, or at least reducing, fight-or-flight mode. And it also forces you to address your anxiety no matter what, even if you don't recognise it as the problem.

Obviously common sense is required here. If your symptoms are very serious and/or worsening quickly and/or people around you are worried, then don't wait 3 weeks to see the doctor! Also, if you're just scared that three weeks might be too long, reduce it to a time frame you're more comfortable with, but try for at least 10 days.

As I mentioned, the three-week rule isn't only useful for health anxiety can be adapted for other types. For example, suppose you are worried that your partner wants to leave you, or your child might be on drugs, or that your company might be going under. Put that big X in the diary three weeks from now (or however long is an appropriate length of time for this particular situation) and promise yourself to revisit it then, and only then, unless something very major changes in the meantime.

Medical Techniques

Very occasionally, we might have bouts of anxiety that are particularly resistant to the types of technique discussed so far and ultimately require a pharmaceutical approach. A lot of people are against taking tablets for anxiety, with good reason. But for others, they are a life saver. The obvious danger is becoming dependent on them, which most of us think would be terrible, but in fact even that is not always the end of the world. If you are lucky enough to not experience any side effects, dependency is obviously far less undesirable than for someone who experiences a lot of side effects.

Normally, though, taking medication to reduce or eliminate anxiety is not advisable in the long term. However, when the degree of terror and/or immediacy is very high, and especially when both are high (the anxiety-causing thing is about to happen, or happening now, and it is causing you huge anxiety), then popping a pill might be the most sensible thing to do. Even if you believe that medication is harmful, you need to weigh this up against the harmful effects that full-on anxiety can have on your system.

The only situation where you might need to look at long-term use of medication is if you have a genuine neurochemical disorder, but as I will discuss in Chapter 5, this is quite rare and you should definitely not accept this diagnosis from your doctor before exhausting all other possible reasons for your predisposition. *We don't want you on tablets for the rest of your life unless you have to be.*

SSRIs and other anti-depressants

There is one thing I feel very strongly about when it comes to conventional medicine as a treatment for anxiety: it should be fast acting. Way too often, especially in some countries such as the UK, doctors prescribe anti-depressants for anxiety. The most common type of antidepressant nowadays is Selective Serotonin Reuptake Inhibitors, or SSRIs. This family includes Citalopram (Celexa/Cipramil), Escitalopram (Lexapro/Cipralex), Fluoxetine (Prozac/Oxactin), Paroxetine (Paxil, Pexeva, Seroxat), Sertraline (Zoloft/Lustral), Fluvoxamine (Luvox/Faverin), Dapoxetine (Priligy) and Vilazodone (Viibryd).

These drugs typically take at least two weeks to take effect (usually four to six weeks), so already that is not much use for someone who is suffering from anxiety *now*. Worse still, *there is overwhelming evidence to show that they can actually make you more anxious*, especially in the first few weeks. Sometimes for that reason, doctors will prescribe you an anxiolytic (anti-anxiety) tablet to take alongside it. SSRI antidepressants also typically require a minimum 6 months of treatment, so your doctor will tell you that you can't stop taking them until you've completed the 6 months. *I'm not a doctor, but this is crazy as a treatment for anxiety.*

As I said earlier, whilst depression is a constant state, anxiety, by its very nature, comes and goes, so this whole SSRI time cycle is not right for the treatment of anxiety. Indeed, many in the medical profession acknowledge this, and say that they are therefore only good for "long term or persistent anxiety". That's basically because they just tend to have a blanket, numbing effect on your emotions, so you might not feel so anxious, but you will also not feel much else, either. Not only that, but there can also be a lot of other side effects, such as weight gain, loss of sexual desire, headaches, sleeping problems, digestive problems and what is called "cognitive dulling"[9], which basically means the person doesn't think as clearly as she used to. Doctors also justify prescribing SSRIs for anxiety on the grounds that "anxiety usually accompanies depression", but the research on this is very ambiguous. Frankly, unless you think you also do have clinical depression, rather than just being unhappy (which anxiety can often make us feel anyway), *I strongly believe that this is* not *the way to go.*[10]

If your doctor tries to prescribe any of these drugs to help you with your anxiety, you should explain that (a) you need immediate help (b) that your symptoms come and go, and most of the time you do not feel anxious (you can be bullish in your definition of "most of the time") and (c) that you only want to take a tablet when you absolutely have to. She or he should then prescribe an anxiolytic (see below), which are specifically meant to treat anxiety. She may argue that anxiolytics are addictive, which many (but not all) are. Obviously, you have to convince your doctor that you're going to be very responsible and only take them as a last resort and allow your doctor to monitor your usage to satisfy you both that you don't become dependent.

If your doctor argues the toss and insists on SSRIs, I would personally advise you to *walk away and find another doctor.*

If you are already taking SSRI antidepressants to treat your anxiety, the situation is more complicated. If you want to change, you will need your doctor's help to wean you off them and there may be a need for an interim drug to help you through the transitional period. Again, do not be afraid to stand up to your doctor and dig your heels in!

There are also alternative techniques that have been used to treat anxiety but that also are probably more appropriate for depression because of their more long-term, ongoing nature. One prominent example is St John's Wort. Likewise, if you currently take St John's Wort, be aware that a weaning-off period will be needed if you want to try something different instead.

---

[9] See for example https://www.ncbi.nlm.nih.gov/pmc/articles/PMC5002481/
[10] Terry Lynch has written very useful books on this subject, including Depression Delusion, ISBN 1908561017.

Beta Blockers and Alpha Blockers

Sometimes beta blockers are prescribed for anxiety. These are normally used to help in cases of irregular heart activity, but have been found to also have an anti-anxiety effect because they work by reducing the action of adrenaline, the chemical that drives fight-or-flight (so that blood pressure is decreased and less pressure is put on the heart). Alpha blockers are similar drugs, used for a similar purpose, and are also occasionally diagnosed for anxiety. Again, I'm no doctor, but logic would tell me I'd rather not take medication that is going to affect my blood pressure unless my blood pressure needs to be treated, so I would prefer to look for other options instead.

Anxiolytics

This is the name given to drugs that are specifically anti-anxiety in nature. There are a number of different classes and categories. Many are now pretty much obsolete, for example, barbiturates, and some are in my opinion a little drastic, for example, opioids.

The most common class of anxiolytics are the benzodiazepines (which I'll call BDs) and those based on them - what are known as their "derivatives". They can be addictive and in high doses, hallucinogenic. Valium is, or was, probably the best-known example. Due to its addictive properties (and perhaps potential for use in suicide attempts), it is not so often prescribed nowadays. Other BDs are less addictive, safer and have fewer side effects. One of the most commonly prescribed nowadays is Alprazolam, better known by the trade name of *Xanax.*

Different people respond better to different BDs and it's important to find one that you tolerate well. Always try a new one on a tiny dosage and monitor yourself very carefully. I hope this book gives you far better and far more effective ways to handle your anxiety than taking BDs. However, I do think there is a place for a packet of BDs in the bathroom cabinet of chronic anxiety sufferers; it can be a comfort to know that it is there, and it can be rewarding to look at that packet and see that you've only had to use it, say once or twice in a year, which hopefully will be the maximum you need after reading this book.

Another type of anxiolytic is azapirones, including buspirone (brand name Buspar). It is a much safer option, as it's non-addictive, not as dangerous in overdose, and has relatively few side effects. However, the down side is that it is slow acting and takes around 2 weeks to start taking effect. So it's more of a medium to long term, daily option. Similarly, pregbalin is a much safer option, but takes around a week to take effect. If you really do suffer with anxiety on a day-to-day, ongoing basis, with no regular low-anxiety or anxiety-free periods, this might be the best option for you.

Alternative medicine - CBD

A natural alternative to conventional medicine that has shown considerable promise in anxiety research and which the World Health Organisation has declared promising[11] is cannabidiol (CBD) oil. Cannabidiol is essentially a cannabis extract that does not contain THC – the part of cannabis that gives you a high and that is addictive. This makes it legal and available over the counter in most countries. Whilst it's a very promising product, one concern is that because it's a relatively new kid on the block, we still don't have much evidence about potential risks and side effects and there may be interactions with other drugs.

Many hemp oils, which are made from the seeds of the plant, contain CBD but in much lower quantities than pure CBD oil.

CBD oil can be taken in many forms, including tablets, under-tongue drops, and by inhalation (vaping).

Weighing up the possible risks, you may consider that CBD oil may be worth a try before going down the conventional medicine route.

In Appendix A I will also look at what else alternative medicine has to offer in terms of treating anxiety. The important thing at the end of this section is that you have access to at least two techniques, perhaps a fulfilled prescription for an anxiolytic and an alternative medicine that you have tested and know will work when needed.

Therapy

Psychotherapy or counselling is also very important in dealing with anxiety, but it's complicated to separate it out as a category of treatment, because different forms of therapy offer solutions which fall into one or more of the above categories. For example, some types of therapy work very strongly as

---

[11] https://www.who.int/medicines/access/controlled-substances/CannabidiolCriticalReview.pdf

a calming technique, others as a strengthening technique, others still as a philosophical technique, and so on. I am going to look at therapy in more detail in relation to dealing with the underlying reasons why we are prone to anxiety, in Chapter 5. However, it stands to reason that having therapy will provide you with weapons of various types in dealing with current anxiety. See Appendix B for information about different forms of therapy.

Completing Your Technique Inventory (Arsenal of Weapons)

We're now at the end of the most important chapter of this book, and *most of the hard work is done*. You should now have learned at least two techniques in each of the treatment categories we are going to use to combat anxiety. Congratulations! Make a note of what you have developed by completing the exercise below, before going on to Chapter 3, where we will start to identify the different types of anxiety that you might experience.

Exercise 14 **Arsenal of Weapons**

Copy and fill in the form below and keep it somewhere safe. You'll need to refer to it throughout the book and in the future, when you have bouts of anxiety.

Treatment Category	My main weapon	My secondary weapon(s)
Calming		
Physical		
Strengthening		
Philosophical		
Practical		
Medical		

Chapter 3: IDENTIFYING YOUR ANXIETY TYPE

In this chapter:
- We'll see how anxiety is not just about worries
- You'll learn to recognise when you have anxiety without even being aware of it
- You'll learn how to look beyond the worries to find out what's really causing your anxiety
- You'll learn what kind of technique will work for each cause
- You'll write your own prescription for treating your non-worry anxiety

Now you have an arsenal of techniques for dealing with anxiety, and each technique belongs to one of six categories. Let's go on to examine the nature of the anxiety you have today, and the likely cause, so that you can prescribe yourself the most appropriate technique from your arsenal for treating it.

If you're reading this book for the first time, you are probably doing so because you are currently experiencing anxiety. So you know you have it. We simply need in this chapter to figure out what is causing this current bout. The thing or things you are worrying about might be the cause, but as I will talk about in more detail in a moment, they might also be symptoms, masquerading as causes. Or you might be feeling anxious but not really know why, in other words, there is no obvious worry associated with it. But there is a third possibility, and one that you need to learn to watch out for, and that is that *you might sometimes have anxiety without even knowing it.*

Unidentified Anxiety

Health Issues

The main message I want to get across in this book is that *anxiety is not just about worries. It is about being in fight-or-flight mode.* When we are in fight-or-flight mode, our bodily functions operate in a totally different way to when we're not, and prolonged or excessive time spent in this way leads to health and behavioural problems. So, you need to know whether you are in fight-or-flight, regardless of whether you think you're anxious or not, so you can manage and treat your anxiety. Also, it's important to become familiar with the possible symptoms of anxiety, both physical and mental, so you can better understand the effects it has on you. The *physical symptoms can often act as an early warning mechanism that you have anxiety*, as they often come before the worrying (if there is any).

Exercise 15 **Anxiety Checklist**

Put a tick by any of the following symptoms and behaviours that you are experiencing now, or have experienced over the last 24-48 hours or so:

Symptom/Behaviour	Tick if recently experienced
Headache	
Backache	
Stiff neck	
IBS, diarrhoea, stomach aches or gastrointestinal issues	
Sore throat or sensation of swollen/lumpy throat	
Shaking, flutters or tremors	
Racing pulse	
Increased blood pressure, especially a sudden "spike"	
Pounding heart or palpitations	
Pins and needles	
Nausea and/or feeling sick	
Acid reflux or increased belching, hiccups or flatulence	
Changes in breathing (rapid or shallow, sensation of not having enough air)	
Unusually tired or weary	
Chest pains	

Difficulty concentrating	
Urinating more frequently than usual	
Insomnia, nightmares or change in sleeping patterns	
Restlessness and/or "jumpy legs"	
Feeling weak	
Sweating more than usual	
Muscle cramps	
Dry mouth	
Feeling of electric shocks in face or body	
Feeling unusually hot or cold	
Earache, tinnitus or pounding in ear	
Dizziness, feeling faint or sense of unbalance or vertigo	
Sense of being congested/sinus problems	
Unexplained coughing	
Unexplained skin rash, being flushed, sense of burning skin, or similar	
General sense of being unwell or developing cold or flu symptoms	
Feeling irritable, bad tempered, angry or snappy, or those around you reporting you being like this	
Feeling sad, down, needy, nervous or weepy, or those around you reporting you being like this	
Generally lacking energy and/or self-confidence and/or enthusiasm to do anything	
Unusual restlessness, can't sit still or relax	
Unusual clumsiness, forgetfulness or absent mindedness	
Feeling of not wanting to go out anywhere and/or socialize	
Change in appetite (increase, decrease or variation)	
Drinking, smoking, popping pills or using other mind-altering substances more than usual	
Having symptoms of allergies (sneezing, itchy eyes or any other type you'd normally associate with an allergy or intolerance)	
Sense of being disconnected from people/the world	
Obsessively thinking about things, going over things over and over in your mind	
Sudden decrease or increase in sexual appetite or desire	

The first thing to notice about this list is just how much mischief anxiety can cause in your body and mind. It's a heck of a list of symptoms and I'm sure there are plenty more besides! Most of us want to conquer our anxiety because we just hate the constant worrying, but this list of symptoms tells you how many other reasons there are as to why it is important to understand it, manage it, and reduce it.

Clearly, not all of these symptoms and behaviours mean you have anxiety and there may be a number of other perfectly good explanations. And please do not avoid seeking medical help if you are concerned (I don't want a lawsuit because people said I told them the symptoms were anxiety!) Having said all that, if you do have any of the above, and especially if you have a few, then you should certainly consider the possibility that they are either being caused by, or made worse by, anxiety. I must repeat this again: *anxiety can exist without worry.* You might not see yourself as an anxious person because you're not a worrier. But if you have these symptoms, it's important to accept that they may be caused by non-worry-based anxiety. Your body is spending too much time in fight-or-flight mode, and this needs to be addressed for the symptoms to go away.

Changes to Sleep Patterns

One of the clearest signs that you are suffering from anxiety will be a change to your sleep patterns. This may be obvious: you are struggling to get to sleep and/or struggling to stay asleep. But they may also be subtler: "needing" fewer or more hours than usual or experiencing nightmares.

Nightmares are a very interesting issue, because if you dream you are in an anxious situation, your body will respond in the same way as if it were real, so your fight-or-flight will be activated, even though you're asleep. For example, if you watched a horror movie just before you went to bed, your sleeping brain may be processing that, and in so doing, triggers your fight-or-flight response. However, it could be that the opposite is true. If you have a very sensitive fight-or-flight mechanism, it may get triggered in the night for many reasons, and your brain might interpret that in terms of unpleasant dream images. In other words, the brain will try to find a reason or build a scary situation, to explain being in fight-or-flight.

We don't always remember our nightmares, and we may be in fight-or-flight while we're sleeping without knowing it. *Waking up not feeling as refreshed as usual is often a sign that you are experiencing anxiety during sleep.*

Recognise the Physical Patterns

Over time, you also might notice patterns of the physical symptoms described above in regard to anxiety. For me, the lumpy throat, neck and back problems, nausea and feeling extremely tired are my most common anxiety symptoms. For the next person, it will be a different cluster of symptoms. Try to recognize yours, because it will help you to quickly identify that you're suffering from anxiety in the future. This is especially important for health anxiety sufferers, because it will help you to avoid/reduce your anxiety that the symptoms mean you have something more sinister! Keeping an **anxiety diary** will help you to do this. On the other hand, if you have different symptoms to those that are normally in your cluster, don't rule out anxiety because your staple ones aren't there. Anxiety is a slippery customer and likes to trick you sometimes.

If the Symptoms Checklist above has revealed that you appear to have anxiety symptoms, or if you have a worry or worries but no physical symptoms, continue to the next section to identify the type of anxiety you have, otherwise go to **When you don't have anxiety** further on in this chapter.

Worry-based anxiety

This is the most obvious reason for anxiety. You've probably got one or more worries that seem to be the cause of your anxiety. You may be like I can be sometimes and have a whole head full of worries. We'll dedicate the whole of chapter 4 to working on worry-anxiety. However, one of the main messages I want to get across in this book is that often, *the worry (or worries) is (are) not really the cause of your anxiety, but a symptom of it.* When we are anxious for any of the reasons discussed below, our brains tend to re-interpret lots of things as worries, that aren't really worries. This is human nature; we associate thoughts with feelings, we look for reasons and explanations for both physical and emotional sensations. *This is hugely important to understand.*

Let's say I secretly gave you an injection that triggered your fight-or-flight response without your knowing. You would start to feel anxious. Then if I asked you "what are you anxious about?" you might say "I'm not sure, perhaps it's because ..." and you'd look for something in your life that might be the cause of your anxiety, and latch onto that. Your brain's now happy because it has an explanation, but it's a bogus one. Try to recognise that state and rather than "finding something to worry about", consider that your fight-or-flight might be caused by something other than this worry.

If what you're worried about doesn't seem to be that serious, or if it's something you wouldn't normally worry about, or if you feel dogged by a whole range of worries, consider that they are symptoms of your anxiety rather than the cause of it, and go through the section below to try to identify the real cause of the anxiety. *Working on worries that are not the actual cause can be a very futile and circular exercise.* (Also see **The Brain's Bogus Worry Exercise** for help on how to avoid this). However, if you're sure that a particular worry is the cause of your anxiety, you can go straight to Chapter 4.

Non-worry-based anxiety

As I've said, worries are often the symptom of anxiety rather than the cause. So in this section we'll look at other reasons why our fight-or-flight response might be triggered.

Sometimes we even find ourselves saying or thinking "I feel really anxious, but I haven't a clue why". Well, that suggests there must always be a thought-reason, a worry or concern, for us to feel it. But this isn't true, we're just made to think like that.

Note that there is some overlap in this list of possible causes with the reasons for being predisposed to anxiety we discuss in **Chapter 5**.[12] For now, we are concentrating on the current anxiety that you are dealing with. We're now ready to diagnose what the likely cause of it is. Having ruled out, or doubting, whether it is a worry, read the following possibilities to figure out what might be behind it, and what might be the best weapons in your arsenal for treating it. Note that the recommended treatments are only suggestions and in any particular situation, you might find that others do the job just as well, or better. Use your instinct and experiment as well.

---

[12] This is because these things can cause a bout of anxiety, but if they are the norm in your life, then they are always going to be there in the background, wearing you down and making you more susceptible to anxiety in general. For example, you might temporarily be on a course of tablets that are affecting your chemical balance and causing you to have a bout or two of anxiety. Or you may be on a long-term course that will continue to increase your likelihood of having anxiety. The former situation may be something you need to just get through and do things to reduce the anxiety you're feeling. The second situation is causing what is described as chronic anxiety and so is something you might need to address in a very different way (change the medication, add anti-anxiety medication, change lifestyle etc). This is covered in Chapter 5.

Response to a threat

Is there something major happening in your life, or a difficult situation you're going through? Bereavement, divorce, change of job, moving home, retiring, a major health issue, major family disruption, being the victim of a crime, going bankrupt, just to name a few examples – or are any of these happening to you or a close loved one? You may not feel worried about it as such, or you may. This depends entirely on the way your brain is wired in general for this particular situation. In a sense, the worrying element of this is irrelevant; whether it's there or not, you will probably have anxiety if you are going through something major in your life.

If worrying is not a major aspect of this anxiety [13], but if you're feeling the physical symptoms of anxiety, then the best thing to do is to focus on things to help you sleep and dissipate the anxiety chemicals that will be flying around your body. So, I would concentrate on physical techniques.

Recommended treatments:

Physical Techniques
Plus, especially if sleep is affected, *Medical Techniques*

Hormonal Reasons

The reason for your anxiety might be hormonal. Are you a teenager or young adult, undergoing post-puberty changes and adaptations? If you're female, do you tend to suffer anxiety when you're menstruating? Or are you perimenopausal or menopausal and has anxiety become a problem (or worsened) as this stage began to develop? Or are you on the pill and has the anxiety become a problem since you started to take it? If you are transitioning, are you undergoing a course of hormonal treatments as part of your gender reassignment? If the answer to any of the above (or similar) is yes, then it sounds like a hormonal issue that will predispose you to anxiety on an ongoing basis. Please look at the section on **hormonal predisposition** for more on this.

If it's none of the above, it might still be hormonal. Some courses of medication can affect your hormones and, well, the human body is a

---

[13] If you are worrying a lot about it, then treat it as a high-appropriateness and high-urgency worry: go to Prescribing your approach to your worry.

61

complicated thing and there can be a whole number of reasons why there are temporary hormonal fluctuations. The best approach to this sort of situation in the majority of cases is probably physically-based. Exercise stimulates the right body chemicals in a healthy way and will almost certainly make this sort of anxiety more bearable, if not overdone. The other good approach in this instance would be something from the calming group.

Recommended treatments:

Physical Techniques
Calming Techniques

Physical/Health Reasons

Having given you a long list of physical symptoms that can be caused by anxiety, here's a curveball: an awful lot of them can be the cause, rather than or as well as, the symptom! *There is real chicken-and-egg issue around physical symptoms and anxiety.* The fact is that anxiety can cause a whole gamut of physical ailments, but equally, every one of them can cause anxiety.

Pain and illness will automatically trigger our fight-or-flight response, just as danger does. If you have a medical condition, especially one that causes you pain, even if it's in the "discomfort" category rather than the "screaming in agony" category, then in all likelihood you will have anxiety as a result.

People with bad backs or persistent neck problems, for example, are probably well aware of this: if your back or neck is "out", the musculature around the injury tenses up to protect the injury. You become very stiff, or "tense", and the brain can tend to interpret that tension as a threat and trigger the fight-or-flight response. The same may be true of many injuries and ailments. What's more, often in anxiety sufferers, especially those of us with health phobias, it can become a vicious circle, where the ailment makes us anxious, the anxiety makes the ailment worse, which makes the anxiety even worse, and so on. Refer back to Acceptance in Chapter 2 for more on this vicious circle.

Some health anxiety sufferers visit the doctor all the time to check that each symptom is nothing more serious. Others (like me) stay religiously away from the doctor because they're scared to find out, scared of the fear they will feel while waiting for test results, or even scared of picking up germs in the waiting room. I think we have to find a balance. Make a note of each physical symptom and observe its pattern. Does it seem to improve when you're in a calmer space? Does it go away after you've had a few glasses of alcohol? Has it gone away when you've been on holiday? If so, then it is probably a symptom of anxiety rather than the cause.

On the other hand, if you think that the physical condition is the cause of the anxiety, then whilst you are treating it or waiting for it to resolve itself, there are things you can do to reduce the anxiety it's creating in you. *Concentrate on calming techniques.* If the condition allows you, also work on some strengthening techniques and if it's causing severe anxiety you might consider anxiety medication to help you through.

If the physical problem causing the anxiety is ongoing, recurring or long-term, it might also be a reason for your predisposition to anxiety, making your fight-or-flight response go off too regularly, giving you Type 2 anxiety rather than Type 1. Read **Physically-caused Anxiety** in Chapter 5 to find out how to address a physically-caused predisposition to anxiety.

Recommended treatments:

Calming Techniques
Strengthening Techniques
If necessary, *Medical Techniques*

Excitement

If you are anxious about something coming up in your life, such as an interview, a party, a holiday, meeting new people, an exam, buying a house or car, consider that anxiety is just one side, or interpretation, of your fight-or-flight mechanism being activated. The other side of this is excitement. You feel anxious because this thing is important to you. If you look at it another way, you can "reframe" this feeling as excitement. *Allow yourself to feel that excitement!* You could be about to get a new job, go to a great party, have a great holiday, make new friends, pass an exam, buy a house or car! It sounds like a very simple thing, but just looking at this sensation as excitement can make it feel positive and worthwhile. This is where we can change the way we think. Those of us who are prone to anxiety will interpret the triggering of fight-or-flight as a negative thing. Say to yourself "My body is in fight-or-flight because something important and exciting is happening in my life. This is a good thing!"

I find I start getting anxious about a week or so before I am due to go on holiday. Sometimes by the time the big day comes, I feel ill and sometimes it's so bad, I don't even want to go any more. This is a situation that's perfect for reframing. Part of the reason that my fight-or-flight response has been triggered is that, yes, there are a lot of worries that can be associated with travelling, because lots of things can go wrong. Will I miss my plane? Will the airport be a nightmare? Will I miss my connecting flight? Will my luggage get lost? Will they have my reservation at the other end or will they have lost it? What if the weather's awful the whole time I'm there? But I need to remind myself that the main reason that my fight-or-flight has been triggered is that I'm excited. My adrenaline is pumping! I'm going on holiday! I'm going to have a great time, see new places, meet new people, eat new foods, let my hair down, relax! I'm going to get to spend quality time with people I love! *Focusing on these positive reasons for our anxiety can really help us to accept it*, which doesn't take it away completely, but reduces it and makes it feel worthwhile.

On the surface of it, being excited is about the best reason for fight-or-flight to be activated, but even that can become a problem if it's frequent or ongoing. Like any other cause, anything that leaves you in fight-or-flight too much will have a negative effect on your health.

So if this excitement is ongoing or part of a lifestyle choice, read the **addiction section** below, as the principles there may apply to you.

Recommended treatments:

Calming Techniques

Overload

Modern society is often extremely demanding. We are bombarded with information, life tends to be very competition-based, and many of us find ourselves juggling way too much, in our work lives, home lives, social lives, and in the practicalities of life, such as commuting, shopping and managing our affairs.

The very weight of "things to do" can cause anxiety, especially for those of us who find it difficult to switch off. My wife gets very frustrated with me sometimes because she will say something to me and there is a delay –

sometimes of minutes, even hours on occasion – before I respond. She believes that I have so much going on in my head that I have an internal air traffic controller, who keeps all my concerns circling around in the skies above my airport in a holding pattern, waiting for their turn to land. The conversation she's started with me gets put in the stack and only gets attended to when the concerns before it have landed.

This sort of mental stacking does not necessarily mean you have anxiety, but it is a definite warning sign. What's worse, and one of the biggest difficulties in handling anxiety, is that *things we do that can reduce anxiety can just get put off because there are just too many other things to do.* We don't have the "head space" to do our yoga, or go for that walk, or to meditate, or even to simply relax and chill. When I had finished the first draft of this book, I invited other anxiety sufferers in my social networks to read it for me and give me feedback. I had about 30 people eager to help, yet only 4 or 5 managed to give me feedback. Most of the others had it in their own holding patterns. Many told me they needed to find head space to be able to read it. And therein lies the problem with overload.

I know it's easier said than done, but if your anxiety is happening because you're just overwhelmed with stuff, you have to resolve and simplify. Do some mental housekeeping. There may be a lot of unnecessary tasks, roles, interactions, emails, social media involvements etc. What adds to your pile of "to do's" that really doesn't need to be there? Have a little cull. Even one less thing to do will create some much needed "head space". I know what you're thinking. You're stating the obvious, Yvonne. If it were that simple, I would have done it by now. My answer is this: *you absolutely need to do this, or your health will be affected.*

With overload we are spinning plates, like those old variety performers from years ago. There are twenty, thirty, forty plates spinning on the ends of poles, any of which will drop if we don't dash to it and give the pole another flick. We believe we don't have time to stop and think about whether any particular plate needs to be there, otherwise they'll all start crashing down around us. So, we just dash around keeping them spinning. This is exhausting and will run us into the ground. It also makes us pretty exhausting to be around and can impact our relationships.

With this sort of anxiety, no one thing on its own is causing any/much anxiety, so you will find yourself saying "I don't need to remove that, it's not causing me anxiety", but remember, just because it's not a *worry* doesn't mean it's not causing *anxiety* (in this case, by being one of many things to have to juggle). I was so fortunate to know the great psychotherapist Arnold Lazarus, who once told me "If you've got too much to do, if it doesn't give you pleasure or money, get rid of it" and I think this is a good test when going down your list of things-to-do and reducing it until it is no longer the cause of anxiety.

When we are suffering from overload, even things that would normally bring us pleasure become a burden, and we can turn them into stresses. "I really must go on Facebook and update my status, people will think I've died!" or "I really need to watch those episodes of the Walking Dead before my hard drive gets full up" – And so on. *You have to let it go.*

Exercise 16 **Overload**

Make a list of all your "things to do" over the next few days. This should include not just work tasks, but chores, hobbies, social things, everything. When the list is complete, circle anything that won't earn you money or that you won't really enjoy. For work tasks, as they all potentially earn you money, circle those that are least important to the success of your work. Now look at each of the circled items and consider whether you can remove them from the list. Try to remove at least 3 things from the list.

Of course, there are times when there is genuinely nothing on the overload list that you can get rid of, it's just all unavoidable responsibilities. If this is the case, then if it is a very temporary situation – and if there's no way around it, then I guess you'll have to go through it. Acknowledge how hard it is and try to find ways to take care of yourself and be gentle with yourself to ease yourself through it (I'm not going to give you too many exercises to do because that will just add to the list.) However, if this is a fairly typical scenario then consider that your life situation is predisposing you to anxiety. *This needs to be addressed more systematically.* See **Situational Anxiety** in Chapter 5.

Recommended treatments:

Practical Techniques

Other pressurised situations

It's obviously not just being overworked or overburdened that puts pressure on us, there are many other forms of pressure. Having to meet targets, work to strict deadlines, receiving criticism, struggling to get or stay pregnant, there are a million and one possible situations where there is no *worry* as such, but there is *pressure*. Often, the best way to relieve pressure is to "blow off steam", so if you think this may be the cause of your anxiety, consider using some of the physical techniques at least once a day until the pressure is off. As in the case of *Overload*, if you find the pressure is rarely off, then consider this to be an ongoing, chronic situation and refer to Situational Anxiety in Chapter 5.

Recommended treatments:

Physical Techniques

Addictions and eating disorders

Many forms of addiction have a very direct effect on anxiety, interfering with the fight-or-flight response. This is not just true of drug addictions, but can also be true of alcohol and caffeine dependencies, eating disorders, exercise addiction and internet addiction, to name but a few. "Adrenaline junkies" are by their very nature addicted to a hormone secreted by the fight-or-flight response.

Consider addiction also as an underlying cause of your ongoing predisposition to anxiety, as discussed in **Reactive Types** in Chapter 5.

Recommended treatments:

Address the addiction/disorder – see also *Addictions and Eating Disorders* in Chapter 5.

Allergies and Intolerances

I have separated allergies and intolerances out from other physical/health conditions because there is a *strong association between allergies and anxiety*, with both being capable of causing the other. Likewise, food intolerances can also set off fight-or-flight. These are reactive conditions that can be managed relatively easily in many cases and this can produce an immediate and significant improvement in your anxiety levels. Consider that this might be the cause on this occasion, and indeed that it may even be the reason that you have a predisposition to anxiety (see **Reactive Types** in Chapter 5.

Recommended treatments:

Treat illness/allergy
Exclusion diet
Calming Techniques

Contagion

They say that misery loves company, and the same can be true of anxiety. The fact is, when we hang around anxious people, it very often rubs off on us. This could be a family member, co-worker, boss – anyone you spend a significant amount of your time with. *Is it possible that one or more anxious people around you are triggering anxiety in you?*

If this is possible, you need to try to think of ways in which you can isolate yourself from that person's anxiety. Try to observe it and take a step back from it. Detach and see yourself in that environment, like you are in the audience watching a movie. How is your character being affected by that other person? Don't underestimate the effect this can have on you. You need to develop ways of insulating yourself. If you are good at visualisations, put on an imaginary space suit, or erect an imaginary force field, to protect you from the toxic vibes they are giving out. Use *calming* and *physical* techniques to help rid yourself of the infection. If your exposure to this person isn't going to end any time soon, also consider that this relationship might predispose you to anxiety on an ongoing basis and read **Situational Anxiety** and/or **Social Causes** in Chapter 5.

Now you might be asking yourself right now, "Is *my* anxiety contagious? Am I making people around me anxious?" Well of course that's possible, but please don't add that to your list of worries. You're going to get your anxiety under control using the techniques from this book, and that will rub off on the people around you. I also talk more about this in **Helping those Around you to Understand and Manage your Anxiety** in Chapter 6.

Relational Problems

Any sort of difficulty in your relationships can cause you either temporary or chronic anxiety. Arguments, controlling behaviour, needy behaviour, codependent behaviour, bullying, manipulative people, secrets and lies ... any sort of problem like this you may have with someone can cause anxiety without there necessarily being any worrying involved. The simple fact is that such situations can leave you feeling threatened or simply just pressurise you. If it's an ongoing situation, refer to **Situational Anxiety** and/or **Social Causes** in Chapter 5. If it's really long-term family stuff, also read up on **Historic Anxiety** in the same chapter.

Recommended treatments:

Calming Techniques
Physical Techniques
If necessary, *Medical Techniques*

Aftermath

Another important question in relation to unexplained anxiety symptoms is, was there something that was causing me anxiety over the past few days, but which is now resolved? If so, it may be that *you are now away from the threat, but for some reason you're still in fight-or-flight mode.* You're like the wildebeest who's really jumpy after the lion attack in case they come back for more. Some people tend to stay in fight-or-flight for a long time after the triggering event has passed (this can be hormonal and/or genetic, caused by poor performance of the brain mechanisms and chemicals involved). It's a horrible feeling because you just can't understand why you're still on red alert when you know you shouldn't be.

Alternatively, you might be out of fight-or-flight mode, but the toll it took on your body still hasn't quite worn off. *The physical symptoms of anxiety often lag behind the anxiety itself.* For instance, if you have to appear in court and get very anxious, one of the symptoms of that anxiety might be an upset tummy. Once you've got an upset stomach, it can take days to settle down again. So, when the day in court is over and you are relieved, mentally the worry has gone away, but the upset tummy still needs time to right itself. So, just because you don't feel anxious, it doesn't mean that a physical ailment isn't anxiety-related.

If you think this might be the case, monitor it over a couple of days to see if your symptoms are subsiding. Health anxiety sufferers in particular should consider this possibility, because worries about the physical symptoms caused by one bout of anxiety might cause more anxiety, which will make the physical symptoms worse still, and you will get stuck in a vicious cycle. *Just give it a few days (set a target date), tell yourself you're not going to worry about it during that time, and try to focus on other things.* When you've reached the target date, check back in with yourself to see if it is still causing a problem.

Recommended treatments:

The Three-Week Rule

Write your Non-Worry Prescription

By now you'll have worked out whether you (a) Don't have anxiety right now, in which case, go to **When You Don't Have Anxiety**, below; (b) Have anxiety that's caused by a worry – in which case, continue to Chapter 4; or (c) Have anxiety that's caused by something other than a worry. If it's the latter, do the following exercise.

Copy and complete the following prescription for Non-Worry-Based Anxiety.

MY NON-WORRY PRESCRIPTION

Probable Cause(s) of Anxiety– tick one or more:

Reaction to threat in the here-and-now
Hormonal & chemical fluctuations
Other physical changes & conditions
Excitement
Overburdened/overload
Other pressurised situation
Addiction
Contagion
Relational problems
Aftermath of a worry
Other (Please state)

Proposed Treatment (as prescribed for the above cause(s) in the section above):

Mixed Worry and Non-Worry Anxiety

Often, one or more non-worry causes might be present in your life and there is also a situation that is causing you to worry. So, which is it? Worry-based anxiety or non-worry-based? And how do you go about treating it? Every situation is different, but as a rule of thumb I would advise that you *focus on the non-worry contributor first*, and then turn to the worry aspect second.

I was recently having a bad bout of menopausal symptoms and had a dispute with my local council in regard to a planning application. I had a bad attack of anxiety. The hormonal effects of the menopause make my fight-or-flight response over-sensitive and it gets triggered very easily. My worry about the planning permission would probably cause me a little anxiety even if my hormones weren't raging, but not to the level that I experienced on this occasion. It was horrible and I didn't handle it well. I was drawn into obsessive thinking about the situation and feeling out of control, angry and upset.

The techniques I prescribe in this book were not having much effect at all. Of course, this can happen – we cannot win every single battle with anxiety, no matter how well prepared we are. But, on reflection, I focussed on anxiety treatments aimed at the worry, such as strengthening and philosophical, and neglected those best suited for hormonal causes, especially physical. I think this is a pattern in me that you might find is in you as well: I just avoid (can't face) the physical techniques when I'm very stressed, which is the very time when I need them the most. I have to recognise this as a weakness in my battles against anxiety and redouble my efforts to force myself down the physical route at those times.

When you don't have anxiety

If you've been through the list of symptoms and don't have any or you are confident they aren't caused by anxiety ... and you don't have any worries right now... congratulations, you are anxiety free today! Acknowledge that. *Pat yourself on the back.* Especially for those of us who experience anxiety a lot, it's important to remember these moments. When we have anxiety, we sometimes feel like we always have it, so *it is important to be able to show ourselves that we don't always have it.* Keep a diary, or record a message to yourself to remind yourself that you do get to feel like this sometimes. In fact, you might surprise yourself as to how often you actually are OK. Also, point it out to your loved ones. Sometimes loved ones can see anxiety sufferers as "constant worriers", which doesn't help our self-confidence. Pointing out to them that you're not a constant worrier and that you are often anxiety-free will be good for everyone.

Finally, ask yourself what the trick is. *What are these circumstances that are helping you to avoid anxiety?* Maybe it is that work is going well, or your partner or child or parent is happy, or that you are getting regular exercise, for example, or a combination of things. Knowing and understanding what helps you avoid anxiety is really important, because you can then work on making sure those conditions are true as often as possible. It's important also because it gives you a hint as to what causes you anxiety (for example, if you think you're not suffering anxiety because your partner is happy, then this suggests that keeping your partner happy might be a regular cause of your anxiety).

All right, we now know how to identify unknown anxiety, non-worry-based anxiety and mixed anxiety. Let's now look at the most common cause of anxiety – worries – in more detail.

Chapter 4. WORRY ANXIETY

In this chapter …
- we'll look at anxiety that's caused by worry
- we'll identify four basic types of worry
- you'll learn what kind of technique will work for each type
- you'll write your own prescription for treating your worry anxiety.

Worries usually take centre stage when we have anxiety. However, the word "worry" represents a wide range of different thoughts, and the right treatment will depend upon the type of worry you have. In this chapter we'll look at anxiety that's caused by one or more worries, fears or concerns. We'll learn how to categorize them correctly and explore what the best approach is in each case.

Once we can identify different types of worry, we can then look at what the best techniques are for each particular type. My method for defining the worry type is to analyse the worry in terms of two dimensions: how *appropriate* the worry is, which combines how awful the feared outcome is and how likely it is, and how *urgent* the worry is, which combines how terrified you are feeling about the feared event, and how soon it might happen.

Appropriateness: Likelihood

Is our worry-anxiety appropriate? Is it an appropriate response to a potential threat, or is it *Type 2 Anxiety* – an inappropriate response to an unlikely event? The first part of this is low *likely* it is. I want you to try to put your worry(ies) on a scale, from, say "50% or more chance of this happening" to "1,000,000+ to 1 chance of this happening".

Note that we're talking here about the *likelihood of the disaster you fear happening*, not the likelihood of the dangerous event happening. You might be 99% certain you're going to fly on that plane tomorrow. But the chances of it crashing are much lower, and the chances of you dying in that crash are lower still. If plane crashes never resulted in injury, would you be so scared of your plane crashing? Probably not. It is the possibility of serious injury or death as a result of the plane crash that is your anxiety, not the plane crashing *per se.* The chances of you giving that presentation tomorrow might be 99%. But the chances of you stuttering and making a fool of yourself, or throwing up on your audience, or fainting or going into a panic attack – whichever is your anxiety-provoking fear – will be much lower.

> *Exercise 18 Likelihood*
>
> *For each of your current worries, try to honestly rate the feared outcome in terms of how likely it is and mark it on the chart below. In all cases, it's the chances of the most feared outcome you need to measure.*

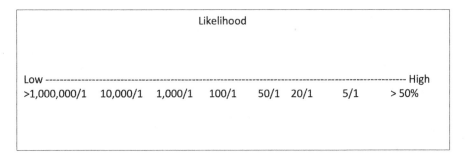

If you have more than one thing that you're anxious about, rate each one of them on the scale and note what each one is (if you are orderly, you can colour code them!)

Your anxiety might cause you to overestimate the likelihood of your feared event happening. If you think that might be the case, ask someone you trust to also give an estimate of the likelihood of it happening, given all the facts. Be open to accepting that they are more rational, but don't let them underestimate because they think they're reassuring you. You're not stupid and it will probably make you more anxious because you'll wonder why they're feeling the need to paint a rosy picture!

Here's my chart based on my worries at this moment:

Activating event 1: Looked at credit card statement and the balance is very high.
Actual fear: I will lose financial security and become very poor.

Activating event 2: I have a cold.
Actual fear: My cold is actually something life-threatening and I might die.

Now I'll plot those actual fears on the likelihood scale:

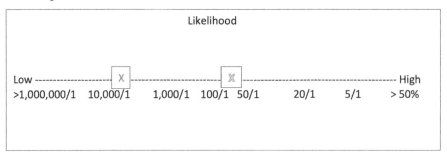

Knowing that something is an irrational fear and very unlikely to happen won't stop us from being anxious, but on the other hand, if *yours is toward the left of the scale, maybe acknowledging that will help a little.*

The fact is that anything to the left of around 5/1 is probably Type 2 Anxiety and not Type 1. Although this will also depend on the worst-case scenario – how serious the feared event is.

OK, so now we have an idea of how likely the feared event is. The more toward the right of the scale, the more likely it is, so we'll call it *High-Likelihood.* In this case, there is less point in applying techniques that attempt to take you out of fight-or-flight and there is more point doing things that will help you get through it. However, on the other hand, the more toward the left of the scale, the less likely it is, so we'll call it *Low-Likelihood*. This suggests a different set of techniques. But don't go off and base your approach on this likelihood scale, because there are other factors to take into account as well (although if you want to, it's there in footnote[14] for high-likelihood and footnote[15] for low-likelihood). For now, just make a note of your result.

Appropriateness: Severity of Outcome

What's the worst thing that can happen? Often with anxiety, it is something tragic. In health anxieties, for example, often the fear is death. There's nothing more severe than that! But other anxieties have less serious outcomes. Sometimes we forget to think through this worst-case scenario question.

Let's say you are going on holiday and are anxious about missing the train or plane, or the car breaking down on the way to the airport. What's the worst thing that could happen?

Look at the anxiety when queueing at the airport gate these days – everyone is afraid that there won't be enough overhead locker space by their seat. What's the worst thing that can happen? Your hand luggage is put in the hold? It gets stolen? Will that really be the end of the world?

My mother-in-law gets anxious about not being able to park. What's the worst thing that can happen? You will drive and drive around and around for ever, until you run out of petrol, then get towed away by the police?

---

[14] In principle, Physical Techniques and Strengthening Techniques should help, and if appropriate Philosophical Techniques as well. The physical techniques will help you to vent your pent-up anxiety, the strengthening techniques will help strengthen your resolve to face the issue and the philosophical approach may help you find meaning or comfort in regard to what you're going through.

[15] In this case, Calming Techniques and Practical Techniques are perhaps the way to go. Calming/relaxation techniques can help you out of fight-or-flight (if the event is not so likely, you perhaps are safe to come out of fight-or-flight) and practical techniques will help you put your worries to one side and focus on other things.

Just as in *likelihood*, knowing that the worst-case scenario really isn't that bad doesn't stop us from being anxious. We're not stupid. We know it's not the end of the world. However, in much the same way, we need to think about it and identify it, so we can then go on to prescribe the best technique for the type of anxiety we are dealing with.

Let's introduce another scale:

Exercise 19 **Severity of Outcome**

Try to honestly rate the feared outcome(s) in terms of how tragic/disastrous it is. Think hard – because your first reaction might be "it would be the end of the world" – but would it? Again, consult loved ones to help you stay realistic. Mark your result(s) on the chart.

Severity of Outcome

Inconvenient--- Fatal

I'm going to do mine again ...

Severity

Inconvenient------------------[X]--[X] Fatal

I will lose financial security and become very poor

My head cold is something more sinister and I will die

We now go through a similar process to the one we went through for likelihood. The further to the right of the scale, the more severe the feared outcome is, so we'll call this *high-severity*. More severe outcomes will require different interventions to less severe ones. At the very end of the scale, for example, there might be your own death, death of a loved one, or even the end of the world as we know it. Approaches that encourage you to conquer your fear or challenge its validity might not be very useful here – whereas they could be extremely useful for issues nearer the left-hand end of the scale.

As with likelihood, these results do suggest particular treatment types (see footnote[16] for high-severity and footnote[17] for low severity), but let's keep going and focus our targeting even more.

The Appropriateness Dimension

Now that we have both scales, we can look at them together to get an overall picture of the appropriateness of our worry.

Exercise 20 **Working out your Appropriateness Type.**

For each current worry, bring together your Likelihood score and your Severity score from the sections above. Look them up on the chart below. The blue wedge next to your description will give you the appropriateness type for your worry.

---

[16] The best solutions for more severe outcomes will probably include Calming Techniques, Physical Techniques and Philosophical Techniques. The calming solutions will help you to find some respite from the anxiety, the physical will help process the adrenaline in a productive way and the philosophical approach may help you find some meaning and peace in relation to what is happening.
[17] Low-severity would suggest solutions such as Strengthening Techniques and Practical Techniques, that can help you put it on the back boiler.

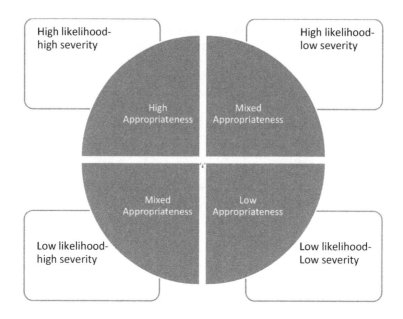

High-Appropriateness

If your worry has high-likelihood and high-severity, then we can call it *high-appropriateness*: it's likely to happen and likely to be pretty devastating, so this is *Type 1 Anxiety*. This is confirmed sighting of lion in the vicinity, and the distinct sound of a nearby roar. But don't panic! It's still just anxiety, you're not doomed. High-appropriateness suggests treatment based on acceptance, but again, we're not going to come up with a final prescription at this stage, because that will depend on the urgency of the worry, which we'll work out below. For now, just make a note of your result.

Low Appropriateness

If your worry has low-likelihood and low-severity, then we can call it *low-appropriateness*. This isn't a judgement. *You're not some sort of failure or weakling if your worries are low-appropriateness, remember, it just means that your involuntary fight-or-flight response is being triggered to easily.*

If it is low-appropriateness, perhaps it's good to think about why that thing is causing you anxiety right now. If it's not the end of the world, and it's unlikely to happen, why is it causing you to be anxious? Often, I find something that I'm not even stressed about sometimes can feel very stressful at other times. The worrying about money one is one such example for me. The fact is that if you have a worry that is low-appropriateness, it may not be a *cause* of your anxiety but a *symptom* of it, as we talked about in Chapter 3. The worry might be bogus, and so expending energy trying to fix it might be wasted energy. The following exercise can help you to identify bogus worries.

Exercise 21 **The brain's bogus worry checklist**

Ask yourself the following questions about your current worry:

(1) Is this the only worry I have right now?
If it isn't, do you have another current worry that's NOT in the low-appropriateness category? If so, it's possible that this other worry may be the cause of your anxiety, and this low-appropriateness one is a symptom of it. The best thing to do in this situation is to put this/these secondary worry(ies) on the back burner and work on the main worry. If there's no obvious "main contender", but you do have a few worries, then it could be that there is a cascade effect occurring. Perhaps a lot of small worries (and/or other reasons) have caused overload and fight-or-flight to be triggered. Or perhaps the anxiety has been triggered by something other than a worry. Go back to **Chapter 3** *and follow the instructions to try to identify the cause and work out how to address it.*

(2) Have I been through something stressful in the last few days that's now resolved?
If yes, remember that fight-or-flight sometimes takes a while to switch off and the physical symptoms of anxiety can take a few days to subside, so your brain might be trying to find a reason for the physical symptoms that still haven't subsided and assigning blame to something that isn't a real worry. See **Aftermath** *in Chapter 3.*

(3) Do I worry about this thing on and off? *In other words, can there be long periods when it doesn't feel like a problem, but then every so often I find myself worrying about it again?*
This is a classic sign that the worry is a symptom of the anxiety and not the cause of it. When our brain looks to attribute the anxiety feeling to something to worry about, it often will go down a familiar route and play that worry again. It's like anxiety's greatest hits album. If the worry fits into this category, put it to one side, go back to **Chapter 3** *and re-evaluate what else might be the cause of your anxiety.*

If you didn't find a positive answer to any of the questions in the above exercise, then perhaps your *low-appropriateness* worry is the cause, rather than a symptom, after all. Sometimes, something just gets under our skin and stresses us, even though it's not that likely or severe. Make a note of it for now and continue.

Mixed Appropriateness

It's also possible that you're high-likelihood and low-severity or low-likelihood and high-severity. Make a note of that for now.

So now we know the appropriateness of the worry, and we can see that we should choose different techniques to treat *high-appropriateness* worries and *low-appropriateness* worries. But the approach you choose will also depend on how urgent the anxiety is. If it's urgent, it's not going to be much help to start reading philosophy books or booking therapy sessions. So, in the next section, we'll look at the *urgency* dimension.

Urgency: Degree of Terror

Fight-or-flight mode isn't just on or off; it has degrees of activation. When the wildebeest hears a rustle in the bushes, she becomes aware, alert. Her fight-or-flight is activated, but at a low level. But when she hears a second sound, or smells something that could be lion breath, the volume of her fight-or-flight will be turned up. Masters of suspense such as Alfred Hitchcock don't (normally) start the movie with the terrifying event, they build it up, slowly, turning on the viewer's fight-or-flight response and then slowly increasing it until it reaches a crescendo. They hold the viewer in a controlled state of fight-or-flight (the very word "suspense" means leaving something unfulfilled).

How anxious are you on a scale of 1 to 10? Is it more of a nagging worry, like at the start of the horror movie, or tension, nagging thoughts in your head, feeling irritable and angry etc? Or are you shaking with fear, having panic attacks or feel sick with anxiety, like when the axeman has just jumped out from behind the curtain wielding the axe? Are you able to function? A score of 10 on the anxiety scale would be that second extreme. The nagging doubts type would be at the zero end of the scale. I'm going to call this scale *degree of terror*.

Clearly, it's important to know your degree of terror when deciding how to tackle your anxiety. If you're terrified or panicky, there's no point trying to do something that requires concentration or study. It's a very different situation from that "rustle in the bushes" type of low-level anxiety, which can allow us a lot more flexibility in terms of how we tackle it.

Identifying where yours lies on the scale will help you to choose the best technique.

---

*Exercise 22 **Degree of Terror***

Mark your current level of anxiety on this degree of terror scale. It should reflect how you've been feeling today, over the last few hours perhaps, rather than at this very instant (because focusing on this exercise might make you temporarily more or less terrified).

Degree of Terror

Mild-- Extreme
(for me)   (Terror)

If your score is toward the left of the chart, it is a *low-terror* score and if it's toward the right, it's a *high-terror* score. Again, these results do suggest particular treatment types (see footnote [18] for high-terror and footnote [19] for low terror), but let's keep going and focus our targeting on one more element.

---

[18] For low-terror, concentrate on Strengthening Techniques and Practical Techniques. The strengthening techniques will help you confront the situation and practical solutions will help you put it to one side and get on with the rest of your day.

[19] For high-terror, concentrate on Calming Techniques, without question. If possible also employ some Physical Techniques_to help your body vent the anxiety in a healthy way.

Here's my completed Degree of Terror scale:

Degree of Terror

Mild-- Extreme
(for me) ⊠ X (Terror)

I will lose financial security and become very poor

My head cold is something more sinister and I will die

Urgency: Immediacy

We can plot each worry on an immediacy scale, from "at some point in the probably distant future" at one end, to "any minute now" at the other end.

As with likelihood, sometimes in order to answer this question we need to figure out what the real feared event(s) is (are). Let's take a health check, such as a mammogram or a prostate exam for example. What is the feared event? That they see something unusual on the x-ray and want to call you back? Or that when they call you back, they tell you it's a malignancy? Or is it the chemotherapy, radiotherapy or surgery that might be needed? Or is it that all the treatment will fail and you die? It might be more than one, or all of these of course, but try to pick the thing that seems to be the focus of most fear.

Why is this important? Well, again, the best technique for dealing with our anxiety may be very different depending on the immediacy of the feared situation. There would be no point, for example, booking a therapy session to help with anxiety caused by something that's going to happen in the next 5 minutes!

Exercise 23 **Immediacy**

How soon is the feared event going to happen, or if it's not definite, when is it most likely to happen? Plot your worry(ies) on the immediacy scale, below. The middle of the scale would be, say, some time in the next 6 months. If it's something that could happen tomorrow, but could also be in 50 years' time, go for "some point in the future". If you don't know, take your best guess, it doesn't have to be all that accurate. There are no right and wrong answers, these are all just guides to help direct us to techniques that are more likely to work.

Immediacy

Some point in--- Any minute
Future   now

Here's mine:

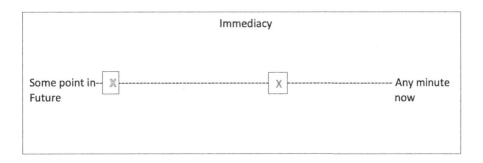

Immediacy

Some point in-- X ------------------------------------ X ------------------------ Any minute
Future   now

I will lose financial security and become very poor

My head cold is something more sinister and I will die

If your score is to the left of the scale, it is *low-immediacy* and if it's to the right of the scale, it's *high-immediacy*. Again, these results can suggest treatment types on their own (see footnote [20] for low-immediacy and footnote [21] for high-immediacy), but let's just make a note of the type and bring back the degree of terror score we worked out in the previous section. Both degree of terror and immediacy relate to the urgency of your situation, so we can combine the two to get an overall level of *urgency*.

The Urgency Dimension

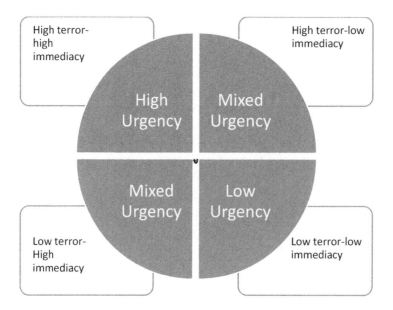

---

[20] For *low-immediacy*, there's more time to employ Philosophical Techniques and perhaps an appropriate course of psychotherapy.

[21] For high-immediacy, use Calming Techniques to help you feel centred, and Physical Techniques. If you have been able previously to train yourself in Visualisations – Developing your Inner Demon and Inner Hero or Self-Hypnosis, use them now.

High-Urgency

If your worry is *high-urgency*, then it's obviously right on top of you, right now, and we need a quick technique to get you down from that horrible place straight away. We'll probably be employing a mixture of calming and physical treatments, but to make an accurate prescription, we also need to take the appropriateness into account. We'll look at them both in combination in the next section.

Low-Urgency

If your worry is *low-urgency*, there will be more breathing space to explore other solutions, but again, we need to cross-reference this with our appropriateness score to decide on the very best approach.

Mixed-Urgency

You might also have a mixed urgency situation, where your degree of terror is high, but the feared situation is not imminent, or the other way around. Just make a note of it for now as we're going to move on to pinpointing our overall worry type in the next section.

Prescribing your approach to your worry

OK, we have a good idea of the characteristics of the worry or worries we're dealing with. Now we need to decide the right type of approach, depending on what those characteristics are.

Our first task is to prescribe the best approach for each worry. (If you've got several worries this might result in a lot of different things to do, but just focus on the main ones, and we'll prioritise them in a minute).

87

There are four main worry types:
High Appropriateness – High Urgency
Low Appropriateness – Low Urgency
High Appropriateness – Low Urgency
Low Appropriateness – High Urgency

In a moment, I'm going to suggest approaches based on these four types. But there are then twelve more types where either appropriateness or urgency, or both, are mixed. In these cases, I want you to decide for yourself which of the four categories best describes this worry. Let's take my worry about my head cold as an example. It's *high-severity* (death!) but *low-likelihood*, so it's *mixed-appropriateness*. And it's *low-terror* but *high-immediacy*, so it's *mixed-urgency*. I think I'll treat both cases as low; it's so unlikely that even though the feared outcome is severe, worrying about it isn't really appropriate. And as my degree of terror about it is low and the immediacy of the feared outcome isn't all that high, I think it's best seen as *low-urgency*.

Plodding through this categorisation process might seem a bit tiresome and long-winded to begin with, but once you've grasped the principle, you should be able to quickly identify the type of worry you're dealing with and just simply look up the recommended approach.

High-Appropriateness and High-Urgency

If your worry falls into this category, then it's serious, full on, and *now*. There is a good chance that the lion is coming for you, it's coming now, and you are on extremely high alert. There's no time to implement any time-consuming treatments. We need to just get you centred and prepared.

Recommended treatments:

Calming Techniques
Physical Techniques
The Anxiety Coach
Anxiolytics

Low-Appropriateness and Low-Urgency

If this is your worry type, then you'll treat this very differently than a high-high. We are talking about something that's not all that likely to happen, that won't be that disastrous if it does happen, your fight-or-flight is not at max level and it's probably not about to happen any time soon. If a low-low worry really is the cause of anxiety rather than a symptom, it's a tricky one to treat, because there must be a reason it's bothering you. You can maybe begin by trying some of the practical approaches, but if it persists, you might want to try talking to someone to try and figure out what it is that makes this worry persist with you.

Recommended treatments:

Practical Techniques
Therapy/Counselling

High-Appropriateness and Low-Urgency

OK, it's not going to happen any time soon, and you're not in full blown crisis about it, but there's a good chance it might happen and it's something quite serious. I would suggest that in this case, a philosophical approach might be best, to help you come to terms with what you are faced with and perhaps to find meaning in it. Given the low urgency of the situation, it might also be useful to have some cognitive-based therapy, to help you to think about it in more productive ways.

Recommended Treatments:

Philosophical Techniques
Cognitive Behavioural Therapy (CBT)

Low-Appropriateness and High-Urgency

This type of worry-anxiety is one of the most common and comes about when our fight-or-flight is in full force about something that would happen imminently, even though it is unlikely to happen, and might not be that awful if it did. What will happen if I get there and they've lost my booking? What if I don't know what to say at the party and nobody likes me? What if I've made a mistake on the order and I've bought the wrong thing? What if I forget my lines? The best approach to this type of worry is to try to strengthen your resolve, to help you face the situation. Some of the practical techniques should also be good as well.

Recommended treatments:

Strengthening Techniques
Practical Techniques

---

*Exercise 25 **Your Worry-Anxiety Prescription***

For each worry you have worked on, fill out a copy of the following form. Find the recommended treatments above that correspond to the worry type in the first part of the form, choose one or more that you think might help with this problem, and write them on the bottom part of the form.

MY WORRY PRESCRIPTION

Complete a copy of this form for each current worry, or the main one(s) if time is limited.

My Worry is (describe in around 10 words or less):

Circle the scores obtained in The Appropriateness Dimension and The Urgency Dimension:

Appropriateness   Low/High

Urgency   Low/High

Proposed Treatment (as prescribed for this worry type in the section above):

Refining and finalising your proposed approach

You should now have one or more filled out versions of the above form based on whether you have one or more worries that you are preparing to tackle. If you have more than one worry, and/or you have a number of different treatments listed, then you might need to prioritise. Follow the instructions in the exercise below.

---

*Exercise 26 **Planning your intervention***

For each of your worries, look at the recommended techniques for that worry type and come up with a plan of attack in terms of what worries to tackle, what techniques you want to try and in what order. When making your choice, think about these aspects:

Priorities
If you've more than one worry, start with those that are more urgent, as follows:
TOP priority: Treatment for High-Appropriateness High-Urgency worries
2nd: Treatment for Low-Appropriateness High-Urgency worries
3rd: Treatment for High-Appropriateness Low-Urgency worries
4th: Treatment for Low-Appropriateness Low-Urgency worries

Don't be afraid to simply tear up the prescription forms for some or most of the worries if you have a lot, and concentrate on just a few (or just one).

Technique Selection
If you aren't sure which technique(s) to choose, ask yourself the following:
Motivation*: Have I got the head space to do this right now?*
Confidence*: Is this something I think will work for this worry?*
Time*: Do I have the time to put in to give this approach a good bash?*
Cost*: Is this technique possible right now for me financially?*

If the answer to any of the above questions is no, try to find an alternative technique from the same category. For example, if it's a physical technique that isn't feeling right this time, try to substitute it with another physical technique. Is there a technique that's not listed for this worry type that you really think might help in this case? Go for it! Listen to your gut and your experience rather than blindly following my guidelines.

This last point is important: *you shouldn't stick to the recommended approaches too rigidly.* You can also look at other approaches that I haven't recommended for your particular worry type and see if they work for it. With practice and over time, you might find yourself disagreeing with a few of my recommendations in general. For example, you might discover that for you, what works best in *high-high* is a philosophical approach. Don't worry, I won't be offended! This is to be expected. It's by no means an exact science and, in any case, everyone is different. As you discover what works for you, personalise and change the recommended solutions above for each type to reflect your experience.

That's it for Chapter 4. You should be walking away from this chapter with one or more forms in your hand, your own self-administered prescription(s) for treating your anxiety. You can now start working on those solutions. Good luck!

I hope you are now feeling empowered and able to diagnose and treat anxiety when it happens. However, we don't just want to be treating anxiety when it occurs. Ideally, we need to figure out why we're predisposed to feeling anxiety too often, or too acutely or for too long in general – why our fight-or-flight mechanism is over-sensitive - and address that, so we can reduce the chance of it happening in the first place. When you feel ready to move on, and have some respite and headspace, head for Chapter 5, where we'll look at the reasons why we're more susceptible to anxiety – that is, why we have Type 2 Anxiety rather than Type 1.

Chapter 5. REASONS FOR YOUR PREDISPOSITION

In this chapter:
- We'll look at what the underlying reasons are that make some people more anxiety-prone than others (their predisposition to anxiety)
- We'll look at the best way to treat each different underlying reason
- You'll write your own prescription for treating your own predisposition.

Now that you know how to target and treat anxiety when it flares up, we can start to drill a little deeper and ask ourselves: *why am I an anxious person?* In all likelihood, the reason you're reading this is the same reason that I'm writing this – we have Type 2 Anxiety. We become anxious too frequently or too easily, or both, without good reason. So, in this chapter we are going to figure out why we are more susceptible to anxiety in the first place and identify the best way to deal with that.

There are so many things that can cause a predisposition to anxiety, for example:
Genetic predisposition
Learned behaviour
Traumatic causes
Hormonal causes
(Brain) Neurochemical causes

Physical causes
Sexual causes
Food intolerances
Illnesses and allergies
Side effects of medication
Addictions and eating disorders
Environmental issues
Situational issues
Social causes
Phobias
Unconscious or unknown causes

Just as we have done with symptoms, if we can figure out what the cause (or causes) of our predisposition to anxiety is, we can then apply the right kind of technique to try to address it (or them).

This isn't as easy as it sounds. Just as the doctor can't always identify why you seem to get bacterial infections so often, for example, we can't always know what is causing our fight-or-flight mechanism to be triggered too much. The doctor might be able to send you for tests to get to the bottom of something. But there are no medical tests, to my knowledge, to tell you the reason you're predisposed to anxiety. That's not so say there might not be in the future – maybe for example they'll discover a gene that causes faulty fight-or-flight triggering. But for now, we're going to have to try to figure it out ourselves, by observing our own patterns and using some good old common sense.

As we are dealing with underlying predispositions here, the kind of techniques we used to treat current bouts of anxiety are, for the most part, not going to be enough to really get to the heart of the issue. In many cases, you are probably going to need make lifestyle changes or change the way you think and behave in response to stressful stimuli. This will often be best accomplished with the help of a counsellor or psychotherapist. Now, I'm aware that many people don't like this idea, or can't afford it, or are sceptical about therapy. Despite my many years in the profession, I'm not evangelical about it, in fact, I once made myself pretty unpopular in the profession by editing a book that highlights problems that clients can have with therapy[22]. But bear with me.

------

[22] Shouldn't I Be Feeling Better by Now: Client Views of Therapy (Palgrave Macmillan). ISBN 1 4039 4740 6. Don't you just hate authors that are always plugging their own books?

One of the reasons why therapy can fail is that it's the wrong type for a particular situation or person. The right kind of therapy for you in terms of your anxiety will depend very much on the reason for your predisposition. *Some schools of therapy are totally inappropriate to some forms of anxiety predisposition.* You could waste a lot of time, effort and money if you don't approach this in an organised way. All the types of therapy I recommend in this chapter are described in Appendix B. Later in the chapter I'll discuss how to go about finding a therapist and offer advice on alternative routes to therapy.

Whether or not you use a therapist to help you, changing your thinking patterns or changing your lifestyle is very daunting and might appear scary, difficult or even impossible. We all have those hackles that come up when faced with meddling with something that has become so ingrained, because we're scared of the unknown world that will face us when we make the change. *As much as we all want to have Type 1 anxiety again, there will always be a part of us that clings on to our Type 2 patterns, because they are safe and familiar.* At this stage, I just want you to adopt a mindset that is *open* to change, even if you're not yet *ready* for change. With that in mind, read on and consider the possible causes for your predisposition to anxiety that are discussed below.

Hereditary Anxiety

Have you (pretty much) always been an "anxious person"? You might not have been as a child, or you might; it might only be in certain situations. Now ask yourself this: Is/was a parent, sibling or other close blood relation also "an anxious person"?

On the day my mother died, she was hallucinating and reliving various moments from her life. The one thing they had in common was they were all times of anxiety. "Be careful, my dog might bite your dog." "Don't eat the head of the carrot, it's poisonous." "Take these and put them somewhere safe so we don't lose them." "Don't forget to ask Mrs Morris to order the food." Maybe this is because she was in an anxious state and her brain was just connecting with anxious memories. But it felt to me that it was a sort of microcosm of her life and demonstrated that her life was lived against a constant backdrop of anxiety. It was also a poignant demonstration of the sadness and pointlessness of inappropriate anxiety; there she was, dying, and yet she was worrying about a food order from 40 years ago, that would never have been the end of the world had it gone wrong anyway.

Given that my sister is also prone to worrying, I would say there's a very good chance that my faulty fight-or-flight mechanism is hereditary. This might be a genetic predisposition - there has been a lot of research into the identification of genes that make you more susceptible to anxiety[23] – or it might be learned behaviour, picked up as a child when we unwittingly copy the model of our parent or other close family member. Adopted children, for example, with an anxious adoptive parent can tend to also be anxiety-prone.

We could perhaps spend a lot of time and effort trying to get to the bottom of whether our hereditary anxiety is actually genetically-based or learning-based, but as any good psychologist will tell you, *trying to figure out how much of a psychological trait is nature (genetic) or nurture (learned) is extremely complicated, and very often there is no clear cut answer anyway.*

Whether it is nature or nurture, *hereditary anxiety* is pretty difficult to shift. It's ingrained in us. If that fight-or-flight response has a very sensitive trigger, it's always going to be that way, no matter what. If this applies to you, it's important to accept that and come to terms with it. However, that doesn't mean to say that there's nothing you can do about it. There are actually two main things you can do – retrain your thinking so that you are sending more positive messages to your fight-or-flight response, and chemically suppress your fight-or-flight response using medication.

Cognitive Behavioural Therapy (CBT) is an excellent tool for retraining ourselves to think in more positive and productive ways and can be a big help when it comes to the worry-anxiety that is part of hereditary anxiety. Perhaps even better for some people is Rational Emotive Behaviour Therapy, because its focus is more generic and gives you tools to use in a wide range of situations. Hypnotherapy is another interesting option. If you are the kind of person for whom worrying is not a major part of the anxiety – in other words, where it is just the trigger going off without any cognitive (i.e. thinking) reason, anti-anxiety medication (anxiolytics) may ultimately be the only fail-safe option for getting you out of fight-or-flight and giving you some peace.

As I said earlier, a lot of people (myself included) are wary about becoming drug dependent and of feeling "less than themselves" if they take drugs on a permanent basis. Others can quite happily take them on an ongoing basis and have no problems. It's up to you, but if we are talking about the rest of your life, it's important to study your patterns, get to know your anxiety and how it works as best you can, so that you become expert at knowing when it can be avoided, when it can be nipped in the bud using other methods and

---

[23] See, for example https://www.ncbi.nlm.nih.gov/pmc/articles/PMC3181683/

when you need to let the medication do its job and turn off that fight-or-flight trigger for a while. More on that in Chapter 6.

Recommended Treatments

Cognitive Behavioural Therapy (CBT)
Rational Emotive Behaviour Therapy
Hypnotherapy
Anxiolytics

Traumatic Anxiety

Historic Anxiety

Was/were there a traumatic event or events in your early life that may have scarred you? Or did you have a very difficult childhood?

A (usually, but not always) early life event or events can undermine your sense of security in the world in general and lead to a lot of anxiety in later life.[24] This could be caused by physical traumas – an accident, assault or bad injury, or emotional ones – exposure to violence, family disruption, bullying, or other forms of neglect or abuse. It could be just one incident, or a more subtle and persistent undermining of your sense of security. There may have been physical or mental illness in your family.

There may not appear to be any connection between these events and your anxiety, but it is possible that they have had an effect at an unconscious level. So it is worth noting that you may have what I will call *historic anxiety.*

Psychotherapy can be very successful in helping us process traumas from the past. Often, a lot of the psychological scarring will exist at an unconscious level, so the best type of therapy might be one which works on making the unconscious conscious, such as psychodynamic therapy. However, these forms of therapy can take years and be very expensive, so they are not always practical. Another possibility if you have the option available in your area is art or dramatherapy, because these non-talking therapies can often access traumatic memories in a more direct way than

---

[24] See for example https://www.ncbi.nlm.nih.gov/pubmed/26163920

through analysis. Person-centred therapy is perhaps one of the next best options, in which your therapist will follow your lead and act as a kind of companion on your own exploration of the trauma. Finally, depending on the type of trauma and your level of awareness of it, some of the techniques developed for PTSD (see below) might be appropriate.

Recommended Treatments

Psychodynamic Therapy
Art and Performance therapies
Person-Centred Therapy
See also those recommended for PTSD (Below)

Post-Traumatic Stress Disorder (PTSD)

If you have been through (or witnessed) a traumatic event, such as combat, a natural disaster, a car accident, or a physical or sexual assault, then you may be suffering from PTSD.

It's obviously normal to be upset, shaky, lose confidence or have trouble sleeping after this type of event, but most people start to feel better after a few weeks or months. If your symptoms are more extreme, or if it's been longer than a few months and you're still having symptoms, you may have PTSD. You can look at it as the fact that your fight-or-flight mode was triggered correctly when the trauma took place, but it's never switched itself off properly again, or the trauma has made it over-sensitive and now it gets triggered too easily. For some people, PTSD symptoms start a while after the traumatic event, maybe months later, or they may come and go over time, even over years.

There are four types of PTSD symptom. Different people have one, some or all four types. The first is flashbacks. This is where you relive the event, via bad memories or nightmares. You even may feel like you're going through the trauma again.

The second is avoidance. You may try to avoid situations or people that trigger memories of the traumatic event. You may even avoid talking or thinking about the event.

The third is negative beliefs and feelings. You can lose confidence in yourself, or in other people, or the world. You may feel guilt or shame.

People can become withdrawn and lose interest in things they used to enjoy, feel numb, or just find it hard to feel happy.

The fourth is being "hyper" (short for hyperarousal). PTSD sufferers are often very jumpy and jittery, constantly in fight-or-flight. They can also flare up easily or indulge in self-harming activities, such as abusing drugs or alcohol.

If any of the above applies to you, consider that you might be suffering from PTSD and that you have *PTSD-related anxiety.*

There are some particular types of Cognitive Behaviour Therapy that are often recommended for treating PTSD. One is *cognitive processing therapy*[25], which is a form of CBT that is aimed specifically at dealing with trauma. The focus is on challenging negative thoughts and interpretations that are associated with the trauma and building a sense of safety. Another is *Prolonged Exposure Therapy*, in which the aim is to reexperience the traumatic event, actively discussing the associated thoughts and feelings with the therapist. It is a type of *desensitization*[26] technique.

Hypnotherapy has also been shown to be very effective in treating PTSD[27].

Another type of therapy that is commonly cited for use in PTSD is *Eye Movement Desensitization and Reprocessing* (EMDR), however, the evidence for its efficacy is somewhat controversial and for that reason I've not included it as one of the recommended therapy types.

Recommended Treatments

Cognitive Behavioural Therapy (CBT) (in particular, *cognitive processing therapy*)
Rational Emotive Behaviour Therapy
Hypnotherapy
Art and Performance therapies

---

[25] See for example https://cptforptsd.com
[26] https://en.wikipedia.org/wiki/Desensitization_(psychology)
[27] See for example http://nvvh.com/wp-content/uploads/2015/12/IJCEH-64-1-05.pdf

Hormonal Types

There are a variety of hormonal changes that happen in the human body over the course of a lifetime. In the modern world, we also have medical treatments that can influence hormone levels in the body. Any imbalance or change to hormone levels can potentially cause anxiety[28].

Puberty

If you are a teenager or you are reading this on behalf of a teenage family member, it is possible that the hormonal changes involved in puberty are leading, or have led, to some or all of your anxiety. For some reason, we tend not to call it anxiety in teenagers – it is often called "teenage angst" or indeed we call teenagers "hormonal" without really thinking through what this means. Teenagers can become withdrawn and sullen, which can seem like depression rather than anxiety.

Think about it – being a teenager is about moving from childhood to adulthood, it is the time of life when we learn to be taken seriously. It is the time of life when we develop sexual interest. Image is important to us, we don't want to look anxious – it's not cool. If we feel anxious, withdrawal and overcompensating with a "whatever" attitude may be the safest way to go.

If this might be the case for you, then you may have *hormonal anxiety*. I should also mention here that there have been studies linking early onset of puberty with increased tendency to anxiety, particularly in girls[29], so this is something to ask yourself as well.

It's not just the raging hormones that can cause teenage anxiety – the transformation from child to adult is scary. The world stops taking care of us to a great extent and we have to start taking care of ourselves, taking responsibility for our own life, not to mention the pressures of exams and so on. So *situational anxiety*, which I'll talk about below, might be occurring as well.

Menstrual cycle

If you are female and in your menstruating years, does your anxiety seem worse at certain times of the month? If so, then you may have *hormonal*

---

[28] For a good analysis of female hormonal life stages and their relationship with anxiety, see https://www.ncbi.nlm.nih.gov/pmc/articles/PMC5613977/.

[29] See for example https://www.ncbi.nlm.nih.gov/pmc/articles/PMC2710300/

anxiety. If you're not sure, try to keep a simple daily record, scoring your anxiety on a scale of 1 to 10, noting the days of your period on it as well. After 3 or 4 months you will probably see the pattern if one exists.

Menopause

If you are female and aged anywhere from around 40 to 60 or more, you could be undergoing hormonal changes as a result of the menopause. The "peri-menopause" period can last a long time, up to a decade, and your hormones can start to change years before the time your periods end, and/or continue to change years after they end. The fall in oestrogen levels that occurs during this period can have a huge effect on anxiety levels.

If your anxiety has become a problem around this age, or deteriorated around this age, then there is a very good chance you have *hormonal anxiety*.

There are also a lot of other symptoms caused by these hormonal changes that can have a knock-on effect. For example, the menopause often causes a poor sleep cycle, and being constantly tired can cause or worsen anxiety. It also commonly leads to joint pain, which can in turn lead to anxiety. These are actually cases of *physical anxiety* (see below), so consider that you might have this as well as, or rather than, hormonal anxiety.

Andropause

The male menopause is not really a myth. It is often overlooked, but men also go through hormonal changes later in life.[30] Testosterone levels can drop quite considerably, although this usually happens more gradually than the hormonal changes experienced by women. But the effects in terms of anxiety can be the same. So, if you are male and your anxiety has started or got considerably worse between the ages of around 45-65, you may be experiencing *hormonal anxiety*. You can have your testosterone levels tested if you want to know more about this; consult your GP if you do.

Hormone-adjusting medication

Any medication that you are taking that affects hormone levels could be a cause of your anxiety (or, in fact, may help it). This can include birth control pills, which directly affect oestrogen levels, hormone replacement therapy, often prescribed by doctors to help with menopause symptoms, the hormone

---

[30] See for example https://www.mayoclinic.org/healthy-lifestyle/mens-health/in-depth/male-menopause/art-20048056?pg=1

therapy undergone during gender reassignment and hormone treatments given to treat "hormonally-sensitive" cancers, including prostate, ovarian, uterine and breast cancer. If you are taking or have taken any of these types of pills, ask yourself whether your anxiety started, or got worse, when you started taking these tablets? Or indeed when you stopped taking them? If so, you may have *hormonal anxiety.*

The fact is that *medication that deliberately changes your hormone levels can be both a cause of anxiety and a solution to it.* For example, in women, both birth control pills and hormone replacement therapy are designed to supplement hormones such as oestrogen and progesterone that are naturally produced by the body. If a lack of these hormones is the cause of your anxiety, taking this type of tablet might help. On the other hand, if you are taking this type of medication for another reason (birth control, heavy periods or menopause symptoms) they might in fact increase anxiety. There is such a complicated relationship between oestrogen and progesterone, the two hormones provided in these tablets, and other hormones and brain chemicals. Also, oestrogen dominance – when the amount of oestrogen is out of proportion to the amount of progesterone – is known to cause anxiety. [31]

If you're not sure whether the medication you are taking affects hormone levels, ask your chemist or doctor.

Treating Hormonal Anxiety

If you suspect you may have any of the types of hormonally-based anxiety discussed above, talk to your doctor. If she agrees that it is a possibility, then you can try either changing or stopping the hormone-adjusting medication you already take or introducing hormone-adjusting medication if you are not taking it. I am not a big fan of hormone replacement treatments, because the interaction between body chemicals is so complicated and fixing one thing can often cause another. But if your life is made miserable by ongoing anxiety, it might be worth considering. You can also try alternative, natural supplements that are known to help with hormonal imbalances. Although bear in mind that "herbal" and "alternative" doesn't mean that it also won't affect your body chemistry in other ways, so research it thoroughly before you proceed.

---

[31] There are some good writeups on this issue at
http://drhotze.com/2017/03/31/much-estrogen-little-progesterone-can-mean-much-anxiety/ and https://www.drnicolerobertsnd.com/articles-1/2017/11/9/estrogen-and-anxiety

For me, if possible, *the healthiest approach to dealing with hormonal anxiety is to stimulate other brain chemicals that counteract the anxiety-producing effects of the hormone imbalance.* Endorphins, Adrenaline, Dopamine and GABA, some of the most important chemicals associated with combating anxiety (see Brain chemistry, below) are all stimulated by exercise. Building regular exercise into your routine will have an ongoing beneficial effect on hormonal anxiety.

A very important thing is to see hormonal anxiety for what it is and thus avoid worrying about the worries it generates. Keeping an anxiety diary will help you to understand your pattern of anxiety in relation to hormonal cycles. This in turn will help you to recognise hormonal anxiety quickly when it happens and see it for what it is, rather than focussing on bogus worries that pop up to give it something to latch on to (also see the Bogus Worry exercise). Person-centred therapy can also be a big help.

Recommended Treatments

Adjust Hormonal Medication – see doctor
Physical Techniques
Person-Centred Therapy

Brain chemistry

Hormones are not the only chemicals in the human body. Another important set are those found in the brain. These are known as neurotransmitters[32]. Problems with the levels of these brain chemicals are directly linked to both anxiety and depression[33]. Many, if not most, modern-day antidepressant and anti-anxiety medications act by trying to adjust the levels of these brain chemicals. However, the association between brain chemicals and anxiety is like the chicken and the egg: is a change or imbalance in brain chemistry causing the anxiety, or is the experiencing of anxiety causing these chemicals to behave differently? *The fact of the matter is that nobody really knows.*

Nowadays it is fashionable to assume that a lack of one of these chemicals – serotonin – is probably responsible for depression and anxiety. This isn't

---

[32] Some chemicals, such as norepinephrine, act as both neurotransmitters and hormones.
[33] See for example https://innovareacademics.in/journal/ijpps/Vol2Suppl1/202R.pdf.

the place to get on my soap box, but I have to say that tablets to increase serotonin uptake – known as SSRIs[34] – are prescribed almost willy-nilly by family doctors to millions of people across the world (one in every eight Americans, for example). Nobody knows, but it's probably only a tiny fraction of those taking SSRIs that actually have a purely physical problem that causes them to lack serotonin no matter what. The vast majority are experiencing anxiety (or depression) for some other reason, and the serotonin levels in the brain are possibly suffering as a result. Or indeed, not suffering at all. *It is extremely rare for this even to be tested and measured* for a proper diagnosis. (I discuss SSRIs also in SSRIs and other anti-depressants)

The chemicals that have a much clearer relationship with anxiety are adrenaline[35], GABA and endorphins. Adrenaline is the chemical that triggers the fight-or-flight response, so clearly, if you have some imbalance of it, it could explain your Type 2 anxiety. GABA (gamma-aminobutyric acid) is a chemical that reduces brain activity, so insufficient amounts will lead to the excessive activity in the brain associated with anxiety (overthinking). Endorphins are released in response to stress, to bring you out of fight-or-flight, so a lack of them will keep you stressing for longer.

Even if you can get these chemicals measured and they are too low or too high, it doesn't necessarily mean you have neurochemical anxiety, because as I said above, this imbalance might be the result of anxiety, rather than the cause of it. However, particularly if you have had long term anxiety that we could not otherwise find a reason for in Hereditary Anxiety or Historic Anxiety (above), that is, you have chronic anxiety of an unknown cause, it is possible that you might have *neurochemical anxiety*. But I would really recommend that you exhaust all other possible reasons before self-diagnosing with this.

Recommended Treatments

Medication – see doctor
Alternative medicine
Person-Centred Therapy

---

[34] Selective serotonin reuptake inhibitors.
[35] Technically, the fight-or-flight neurotransmitter is norepinephrine, which is closely linked with a hormone called adrenaline, but for simplicity here I have considered them as one and the same.

Physically-Caused Anxiety

In Chapter 3 we talked about how bouts of anxiety can be brought on by physical conditions, injuries or illnesses. But if the physical problem is not temporary, that is, if it's an ongoing problem, then could it be the reason you have Type 2 anxiety? Could it be the reason for your predisposition?

Analyse ongoing or recurring physical problems and think about their potential to cause anxiety (especially if there are no obvious other reasons for your predisposition to anxiety). Could this be the cause? Be a detective. Talk to your doctor if you need to, and/or a therapist, to try to get to the bottom of it.

As I said above, pain will automatically trigger our fight-or-flight response. An obvious flag would therefore be any ongoing condition that causes discomfort or pain. If you have such a condition, then consider that you might have *physically-caused anxiety.*

Sometimes, those of us with Type 2 anxiety are so aware that we are worriers that we believe physical symptoms are caused by anxiety, when in fact it might be the other way around. For example, your bad back could be caused by sleeping on a poor mattress rather than by anxiety, and therefore might be the cause of, rather than a symptom of, anxiety. Imagine that - all this worry has actually been caused by your mattress!

Any ongoing ailment that causes you discomfort or pain may be a major cause of your predisposition to anxiety. The balance between go-about-your-business mode and fight-or-flight mode is directly affected by an illness ,as the body mobilises its resources to deal with the problem. It's particularly important in this case that you have a good preventative routine in place to manage your anxiety on an ongoing basis (see Chapter 6).

(I will also refer to reactive forms of anxiety such as Food Reaction and Allergies below, which can lead to palpitations, chest pain, and conditions such as IBS, which might all be chalked up as symptoms of your anxiety when they are in fact causes of it).

In terms of treating a predisposition to anxiety that is caused by physical issues, of course, the more successful you are in managing the pain and discomfort caused by the physical issue, the less anxiety you should experience. It is also very important to address the physical tension and side effects caused by the ailment, as these also encourage the fight-or-flight response. Use Physical Techniques as part of a regular, ongoing routine.

Sexual Anxiety

A strong connection has been established between sexual difficulties and anxiety[36]. Sexual difficulties (or dysfunction) include such things as lack of sexual desire, inability to have or maintain an erection, inability to orgasm or conditions where there is a permanent state of arousal (hyperarousal). *There is an intimate relationship between sex and fight-or-flight.* Men need to be in go-about-your-business mode rather than fight-or-flight mode to get an erection, but they need to be in fight-or-flight mode to have an orgasm. The pattern in women is more complex in terms of arousal, but the same in terms of orgasm. So, you can imagine how sexual appetite and activity can have a major effect on anxiety and vice-versa.

Ongoing issues with sexual dysfunction can be the cause of anxiety, both due to their effect on the triggering of fight-or-flight and to their causing worries – about performance, disappointing one's partner etc. It can also naturally lead to a great deal of physical and emotional frustration which can further fuel anxiety. It's a complicated issue, but it is worth considering that if you do have sexual difficulties of some kind, they may be the cause (or a contributing cause) of your anxiety.

Recommended Treatments

Address sexual issue (medically and/or via sex counselling)
Person-Centred Therapy
Couples, family or relationship counselling

---

[36] See for example http://www.psychiatrictimes.com/anxiety/relationship-between-anxiety-disorders-and-sexual-dysfunction/page/0/1

Reactive Types

Food Reaction, Intolerances and Diet

Food and drink are often overlooked as causes of mood changes, depression and anxiety. Many people are unaware of their reactions to certain foods, and/or the lack of certain food groups in their diet. One example that we've probably all heard about these days is gluten intolerance. Studies have shown that up to 40% of "celiacs" (people with gluten intolerance) report anxiety problems[37]. Obviously, then, if you have a gluten intolerance, there may be a 40% chance you have *reactive anxiety*. But there are many others as well; food dyes, corn, eggs, cane sugar and soy have all been scientifically shown to cause anxiety.[38] Inappropriate changes to our blood sugar levels also cause anxiety, and these are, of course, governed by what we eat. If you go on a chocolate binge, your blood sugar will go up (and you might be on a high) but then go rapidly down, and amongst other things, this can make you feel anxious (it's like a mild version of a drug addict's "come down").

Caffeine and nicotine are both "stimulants", which means that they raise the level of nervous activity in the body. In other words, they put you in (or move you nearer to) fight-or-flight mode. Alcohol, on the other hand, is commonly believed to be a depressant (this doesn't mean it makes you depressed, it's just the opposite of stimulant, and means it has a calming or sedative effect). It moves you away from fight-or-flight to your nice calm place. But before you go reaching for the wine bottle, unfortunately it has been shown that alcohol can also act as a stimulant. This is because it also is addictive, and any addiction can lead to anxiety, because of the dramatic effects overuse has on the body, and also due to the simple fact that we can be very anxious when we can't have the thing we're addicted to!

We are all different, so if there's something you eat or drink regularly, and your anxiety seems to be tied in with when you eat it, then it doesn't matter if there's nothing on the internet about it or whether your doctor thinks it's unlikely. Humankind is only just scratching the surface of science and for every one thing your doctor knows, there are probably a million things she (and science in general) don't know!

Just consider whether what you are eating and drinking on a regular basis might be capable of causing anxiety. If so, you may have *food reactive*

---

[37] See for example
https://www.researchgate.net/publication/326240384_Psychiatric_Comorbidity_in_Children_and_Adults_with_Gluten-Related_Disorders_A_Narrative_Review
[38] See https://www.ncbi.nlm.nih.gov/pmc/articles/PMC4146781/

anxiety. Do the exercise below. It might also be helpful to talk to a nutritionist.

---

*Exercise 27 **Food Diary***

Keep a food (and drink) diary and also note your anxiety levels in the diary. Give them a mark out of 10 each day, or even morning, afternoon and night. You might have to keep this up for 2 months or so. Look to see if there's a food or drink that seems to pop up regularly with a higher anxiety score on the same or next day.

Recommended Treatments

Food diary (see above exercise)
Change diet
Consult nutritionist
Person-Centred Therapy

Allergies

As I mentioned in Chapter 3, allergies and anxiety often co-exist and both can cause the other.[39] Worse is that you might have either, or both, without even being aware of it. It is worth considering whether you may have ongoing allergic conditions that are causing your fight-or-flight response to be triggered too easily.

If there is a possibility that this might be the case, you might want to try a course of antihistamines for a couple of weeks and monitor your anxiety levels (and any recurring physical symptoms). If there seems to be an improvement, then the chances are that the allergy is at least one cause of your anxiety. If it's an unknown allergy, you can then go to an allergy clinic to find out what you are allergic to and find the right way to treat it.

See also Environmental Anxiety in regard to allergies.

---

[39] See for example https://www.thescienceofpsychotherapy.com/allergies-driving-anxiety/

Side effects of medication

It may be that prescribed or over-the-counter medication you take regularly might be capable of causing anxiety. Check everything online or with you doctor to see if this might be the case. If so, you may have *drug reactive anxiety.*

As I have already mentioned, but cannot stress enough, if you take antidepressants, something you should bear in mind is that there is a lot of evidence that they can actually cause anxiety, even those that have been prescribed to help with anxiety. There is a particular issue with what are known as SSRIs – selective serotonin reuptake inhibitors. As noted in SSRIs and other anti-depressants and in Brain chemistry (above), people in the medical profession generally agree that these can temporarily cause an increase in anxiety in the first few weeks, but many people believe that this can also be a long term effect. In my experience, people who start taking these drugs are scared to stop and get into a pattern of changing the dosage, changing the specific SSRI or supplementing them with other drugs, rather than trying a completely different approach.

In addition to anti-depressants, there are many other types of regular medication that can cause anxiety. Consider this possibility and that you might be in a vicious cycle of *drug reactive anxiety.*

Recommended Treatments

Change medication

Addictions and Eating Disorders

As I talked about in Chapter 3, anxiety is a very likely symptom of an ongoing addiction or eating disorder. Whilst you probably don't want to admit it, you *must* consider whether this might be the case. This is such a broad category and to discuss how to treat addictions would require a book on its own, but don't brush this possibility under the carpet: if you don't get help with the addiction, nothing I can offer in this book will ultimately be able to stop the anxiety from deteriorating. If there's even a small chance that an addiction or eating disorder may be causing an anxiety problem, please try to consider it, even though you won't want to admit it. Find a support group, online forum or therapist to explore the possibility further.

Recommended Treatments

Manage/treat addiction
Person-Centred Therapy

Environmental Anxiety

This category includes anything that is in your normal environment – work or home – that might lead to anxiety, either directly or indirectly. For example, if your neighbour has a dog that barks all day, or you work in a noisy workshop, or you live by a wind farm that makes that humming noise, anything that might "get on your nerves" could be a direct environmental cause of anxiety. Likewise, if you work among chemicals – paints, cleaning products, etc – inhaling these chemicals might cause anxiety. Anything in your environment that causes allergies can cause anxiety, and as I said above, there is a very strong association between allergy and anxiety: both can trigger, or at least worsen the other. Think about both your home and work environment and to both direct and indirect potential causes of anxiety.

Also included in this category is anxiety that occurs as a result of SAD or seasonal affective disorder, which is a pattern of mood change occurring at certain times of the year, or in certain prolonged weather conditions. Does your anxiety seem worse in the late autumn, for example, as the days become shorter and darker? Have you noticed it increasing when there are long periods of cold or wet weather? If you think any of these might be having an effect, you may have *environmental anxiety*.

Situational Anxiety

This is a pretty broad category and difficult to pin down, but it basically is where the cause of the anxiety is something that is happening in your life. Let's say you're in a really stressful job. The clue is in the description! If you're in a really stressful job, and you have anxiety, then it's almost certain you have *situational anxiety*. But what if you hate your job, but it's not stressful? You just hate it. You don't like the people, the work is boring, or you feel unfulfilled, overlooked for promotion ... if something is making you unhappy on an ongoing basis, then this might well lead to anxiety. If you're not sure, look for clues. For example, if you work Monday to Friday, do you regularly find yourself struggling with anxiety on a Sunday evening? Do you feel anxious toward the end of a holiday period? Do you sometimes find it very hard to relax at the start of a holiday? You might have *situational anxiety*.

Of course, stressful situations can also lead to anxiety. Some of these are very well known – moving house, bereavement (or illness of a loved one), preparing for a wedding, changing job (or being at risk of losing your job), being in trouble with the law (or fear of being in trouble), personal injury or illness, having children (or preparing to have children) or being unable to have children, unplanned pregnancy or abortion, retirement, change in financial circumstances or financial worries generally, taking exams or being the victim of a crime, for example. Yours may not be listed here. But if there is some *ongoing* issue that is causing your anxiety, where before you didn't suffer from anxiety or had very little, then you may have *situational anxiety*.

Some situations are obviously avoidable, and some are not. *However, if you are in an unavoidable situation that causes ongoing anxiety, then you need to seriously look at ways to make the unavoidable avoidable*, because long-term exposure to anxiety will take its toll on your mental and physical health and may well have a knock-on effect on your relationships. For example, if your job is the situation causing you anxiety, whilst it may seem that a change in job or career is impossible, you might need to face up to the fact that it might be the lesser of two evils. Making difficult life changes can seem very daunting; money often becomes a factor ("I simply can't afford to walk out of my job/career", "I wouldn't be able to pay the mortgage and I'd lose my house"...) Therapy can be extremely helpful in deciding the best way forward.

Recommended Treatments

Manage/resolve situation
Rational Emotive Behaviour Therapy
Person-Centred Therapy
Existential Therapy

Social Causes

I'm not talking here about social anxiety, which is a term often used to describe a phobia (see below) where the person becomes anxious in social situations. This section deals with the possibility that the cause of your predisposition to anxiety might be due to relationships with other people. For example, if you are in a toxic relationship where you're scared of upsetting the other person, you live life "walking on egg shells" – your finger will always be on the fight-or-flight trigger in case they kick off. If you are going through the break-up of a long-term relationship, it will probably cause you ongoing anxiety (even if you are the instigator: it's a big disruption to your life, which can be stressful). Or perhaps you are in a relationship that is too oppressive, too controlling, too one-way, co-dependent[40], or that in any way feels unhealthy? Or you may have ongoing contagion (see Contagion), disruption in your family situation: arguing in the family, people leaving, or elsewhere: bullying, stalking ... If it's ongoing, it may lead to a hyper-vigilance, an itchy fight-or-flight trigger finger, in other words, you may have *socially-caused anxiety*.

This is a cause which, if ongoing, will seem daunting to change. I can recommend therapy to help resolve this relationship issue, but it is possible you will feel resistance against going down that road. What if therapy makes us confront the fact that we need to get away from that person? Life as we

---

[40] According to everydayhealth.com, "Codependency can be defined as any relationship in which two people become so invested in each other that they can't function independently anymore .... Your mood, happiness, and identity are defined by the other person."

know it would fall apart! How many lives would be turned upside down? What would that person do to us if we tried to change things? Or what would we do to ourselves if we had to live with that guilt? We're all scared of the upheaval that therapy might cause, but nine times out of ten, a decent therapist will be able to help you to fix your relationship to make it better for everyone. Therapy should be the best way of saving your relationship, because unless you confront the problems, you can't fix them. Burying your head in the sand leads to more and more problems, and your anxiety is one of them. Get help, trust the process, trust yourself, *feel the fear and do it anyway.*

*Exercise 28 **Relationship Anxiety Checklist**[41]*

You can complete this exercise for any relationship which you think might cause you anxiety. For each of the following statements, give a score from 0 to 3, where 0 is disagree or not applicable; 1 is slightly agree; 2 is mostly agree and 3 is strongly agree.

Statement No.	Statement	Score (0 – 3)
1.	It is hard for me to be happy if this person is unhappy.	
2.	I find it difficult to do things without this person being involved.	
3.	I feel guilty or scared if I disagree with this person.	
4.	I always put this person's needs before my own.	
5.	This person has a lot of control over my life.	
6.	I find it hard to maintain other relationships without this person's involvement or approval.	
7.	I feel controlled by this person's moods.	
8.	It is hard to express any negative feelings toward, or say no to, this person.	
9.	This person would not cope without me.	
10.	I would not cope without this person.	
11.	I feel that whatever I do, this person does not think it is (or I am) good enough.	
12.	This person undermines my confidence or discourages me when I try to do new things.	
13.	This person has a big say in how I look, dress and behave.	
14.	This person can be very critical of my personality.	
15.	I sometimes worry this person will hurt themselves or me if I upset them.	
	TOTAL SCORE	

---

[41] This exercise is intended for reflection and consideration only; it is not a validated scale in any scientific sense.

The maximum score is 45. There are no hard and fast interpretations of these scores, but I'd say anything over 15 means you should consider that this relationship might be a predisposing cause of your anxiety. Anything on or over the 25 mark I'd say it's almost certain. The questionnaire is worded to try to capture both abusive and codependent relationships; you'll probably know which yours is. *It's really important that you start to work on the issue*, ideally with the help of a therapist, but if not, try to talk to friends or join an online self-help forum, for example.

This exercise is more geared to family relationships than, say, workplace relationships (although most questions can apply to both), so even if this questionnaire doesn't really apply, consider that you might still have *socially caused anxiety*. Finally, ignore the overall score for a minute and look at any statement where you have scored anything but a 0. Think about that and what it might imply for you and your anxiety, and whether it is something that you need to work on.

Recommended Treatments

Person-Centred Therapy
Psychodynamic Therapy
Couples, family or relationship counselling

Phobias

Obviously, phobias cause anxiety, because by definition, a phobia is an extreme fear and extreme fear causes anxiety! In terms of anxiety, though, some phobias are more manageable than others, because they do not present themselves on a regular basis. If you have a fear of drowning, for example, it probably won't affect you in your everyday life unless you work on or around water. Your fear of snakes is unlikely to cause you anxiety unless you are likely to be around snakes. However, other phobias are more present in our everyday lives. As I mentioned above, a social phobia (or social anxiety), where you're afraid of meeting new people, or being in a group situation is probably going to rear its head quite often and may therefore lead to a more ongoing or recurrent state of anxiety. A health phobia will also rear its head regularly, as health phobics tend to be very attuned to their bodies and will notice every little pain or twitch or cough or sneeze or sensation and fear that they are sick. Phobias such as enclosed spaces, open spaces and driving are hard to avoid and probably therefore cause us regular anxiety. If any of this applies to you, you may have *phobic anxiety*.

Because phobias are so stressful, a lot of people become anxious about triggering their phobia(s). You can be constantly worried that you might not be able to cope with the phobia if it happens. *We become scared of our own anxiety: we have anxiety phobia!* When this happens, it's horrible, because it's a vicious circle (see Acceptance). "I'm scared I'm going to faint with anxiety/have a panic attack/throw up when I have to give that presentation" or "I'm scared if I am diagnosed with cancer, I am going to have a nervous breakdown". If this sort of thing might apply to you, you have what I call *metaphobic anxiety* ("meta" just means that it refers to itself).

Recommended Treatments

Cognitive Behavioural Therapy (CBT)
Rational Emotive Behaviour Therapy
Existential Therapy
Hypnotherapy

Unconscious or Other Types

If you've got this far and just don't know what causes your anxiety, then it is possible that the reason is buried in your unconscious. You may have repressed it (pushed it from your conscious to your unconscious because it is too painful to deal with), you may be in denial (subconsciously not wanting to admit that the cause of the anxiety is really a problem), or for whatever other reason (because I'm not going to get too Freudian on you) you may just have forgotten it. It is possible, for example, that you are in a relationship or situation that is fundamentally not right for you, but you feel it is unavoidable or have "cooked your goose", so you have buried your doubts and convinced yourself it's fine. Or it may be that something that happened in the past left an emotional scar on you, that you've buried in your unconscious, but it is still having an effect on you without you knowing it. It's really important, and you have to be really brave, to just consider the possibility that this might be the case, and that you might have *unconscious anxiety*.

Recommended Treatments

Person-Centred Therapy
Psychodynamic Therapy
Existential Therapy
Art and Performance therapies

All right. If you're still reading and I haven't covered any of the possible causes of your anxiety, then it is caused simply by something you know about, but I've not included. Let's call this *other anxiety*. Well, sorry, but I can't think of everything! However, do not close the book yet, because whilst it's going to be hard to direct you to the right technique for the cause of your anxiety, it's not impossible. Maybe you can figure out which of those I've covered is most similar to yours and look up the proposed techniques for that. Finally, please email me and tell me what it is I've missed, so I can include it in the next edition!

Treating the Reason for your Predisposition

Do the following exercise to draw up your prescription for dealing with the thing(s) that you think might be what predispose you to anxiety. If you have more than one suspected reason, you might need to prioritise, because it's probably not practical to treat them all at once. I would suggest starting with any types where the solution is relatively easy to apply. Here's my *rule-of-thumb suggested priority list*, from easiest to treat to hardest to treat:

> Reactive
> Situational
> Hormonal
> Social
> Phobia
> Unconscious (unknown)
> Traumatic
> Brain Chemistry
> Hereditary

Of course, this list of what's easiest is a big oversimplification on my part and in reality, it depends on so many factors. You may have very good reasons for prioritising one over another, but all things being equal, I suggest using this method as a starting point.

Based on the priorities you choose, look up the recommended treatments and choose one or more that you would like to try. Put them on the form under "Proposed Treatment(s)". As I said at the start of the chapter, because we are dealing with ongoing and often ingrained predispositions to anxiety, some pretty in-depth work may be required. For this reason, a lot of the proposed treatments involve therapy. In the next two sections I'll talk about the idea of having therapy in general, and alternatives to it if it's not possible or desirable.

Exercise 29 Your Predisposition Prescription

Copy and complete the following form according to the possible reasons for predisposition that you identified in this Chapter:

MY PREDISPOSITION PRESCRIPION

Suspected Reason(s) for Predisposition to Anxiety (tick as many as appropriate but concentrate on most likely/obvious):

Hereditary
Traumatic – Historic
Traumatic - PTSD
Hormonal
Brain Chemistry
Reactive – Food reaction, intolerances and diet
Reactive – Allergies
Reactive – Side Effects of Medication
Reactive – Addictions and Eating Disorders
Reactive - Environmental
Situational
Social
Phobia
Unconscious (unknown)
Other (state here if known)

Proposed Treatment(s):

You now have written your own prescription for treating your predisposition to anxiety.

Going the Therapy Route

If you choose to have some therapy to reduce your predisposition, *it is really important that you choose the right kind of therapy for the reason(s) for the predisposition that you've identified.* Some types are much more likely to be beneficial in some circumstances than others. In completing the prescription form, you have chosen what you think will be the most appropriate approach. If you've got more than one suspected reason, you might be faced with prescribing yourself more than one type of therapy. This is unlikely to work in practice, and the therapists probably won't advise it, so I would suggest going with the one that feels more appealing, or with the greatest choice of therapist in your area, or again, which is the cheaper and/or quicker option.

When choosing a therapist, please make sure you interview a few before making your decision. *Don't be afraid to ask a lot of questions* to find out about their experience, qualifications, methods, fees and conditions and above all, how they would approach your work together. People often feel scared to interview therapists. You might think "who am I to question this professional?" But it's not insulting, in fact, it's irresponsible *not* to do it. Explain to your potential therapist that you are wanting to work on your *underlying predisposition* toward anxiety and your *suspected reason*(s) for it, and see what she says.

The most important element of the therapeutic relationship is the relationship. Above all, it needs to be someone with whom you feel comfortable and in whom you have confidence. I'd rather you were with someone who met those criteria, but who doesn't offer the type of therapy prescribed here, than the other way around. There has to be a rapport for it to work (even to some extent in the case of Psychodynamic therapy) and you really need to hear the person describe their approach to gauge whether it feels right to you. Despite all our training and qualifications, we therapists are *not* doctors or scientists. We *don't* know better than you. We have just learned lots of techniques that can sometimes help, just like you're doing now in reading this book.

Another thing to bear in mind when finding a therapist is that there are a lot more of some types than others. Person-Centred Therapy and Cognitive

Behavioural Therapy (CBT) practitioners are both likely to be much easier to find in your area than some of the other types. You might find that the type recommended for your likely Reason for Predisposition is not available to you.

A lot of therapists nowadays offer a blend of different techniques (they sometimes call themselves "eclectic"). For example, you might not find an existential therapist, but you might find a therapist who can apply an existential approach. But if you have the choice, are you better off with a "purist" who sticks to one type of therapy, or to an "eclectic" therapist? There's no easy answer to that; purists might not be able to adapt according to your needs, but eclectics might be less likely to have very deep experience of the particular type you want to try. Again, ultimately, let your confidence in the person and what they say about their approach help you decide.

IMPORTANT. Just as a final comment on therapy, always be aware that therapy does not always help and even in some cases can actually make you feel worse. Never continue therapy which feels wrong in any way, and *absolutely never where you start to feel you are becoming even slightly dependent on the therapist.* Never be afraid to stop, or talk to your therapist about your doubts, and if that's not fruitful, talk to another professional. Or write to me. Trust your instincts. *Not only are therapists not doctors or scientists, they are also not psychics or gods and get things wrong sometimes.* In fact, not just sometimes – a lot! Therapy can be amazing and help you to transform your life, but that's always more due to the client and her relationship with the therapist than to the therapist himself. For whatever reason, and usually not due to either the therapist's or the client's fault, it does *not always help.*

Going the Non-Therapy Route

If the idea of therapy doesn't appeal to you or is impractical for some reason, then you may be able to be your own therapist. Research the type of therapy you've prescribed above and see if you can find books, internet groups or self-help courses that can train you in the principles of that therapy type. This is more likely to be successful for perhaps Cognitive Behavioural Therapy (CBT), Rational Emotive Behaviour Therapy, Art and Performance therapies (some) and Existential Therapy and unlikely to be practical with Psychodynamic Therapy, Dramatherapy (see Art and Performance), Hypnotherapy (although you can try the self-hypnosis techniques discussed in Self-Hypnosis), Person-Centred Therapy and Couples, family or relationship counselling.

Another non-therapy option is to use Medical Techniques, but as I discuss in Chapter 2, long-term pharmaceutical treatment of anxiety is not ideal and for most people should only be considered as a last resort.

Whilst you're working on resolving your underlying predisposition, continue to treat any current anxiety according to the methods you learned in Chapter 4. This will also help in the overall treatment of your underlying condition.

So, now you have a prescription for treating your predisposition, and have written at least one prescription for treating a current bout of anxiety. You are now starting to understand your own patterns and have tools to deal with anxiety when it flares up. But wouldn't it be better if it didn't flare up in the first place? In the next chapter, we'll look at preparing for and preventing anxiety and things you should build into your lifestyle to keep it to a minimum.

Chapter 6. PREVENTATIVE TECHNIQUES AND HEALTHY HABITS

In this chapter:

- We'll look at what you need to put in place to monitor your anxiety levels
- You'll develop a routine to keep anxiety at bay
- You'll prepare a first aid kit in case you get anxiety
- You'll learn to help those around you to understand and help manage your anxiety.

Anxiety is like any other health issue: by understanding it and what causes it, we can build into our lives good healthy habits that can help us to manage our anxiety and reduce how often it flares up, how long it lasts when it does flare up and also reduce the misery it causes when it does.

Basically, what you need to be able to do in order to manage your anxiety on an ongoing basis is the following:

1. Develop an arsenal of weapons you can use in any anxiety situation, as you did in Chapter 2.
2. Undertake regular and ad-hoc anxiety-busting activities.
3. Regularly monitor your anxiety levels.
4. Learn to recognise the patterns and likely triggers that can cause anxiety.
5. Learn to recognise the physical warning signs.
6. Work on what you've found to stop anxiety before it starts or deal with it quickly and efficiently.

7.   Help those around you to understand and manage your anxiety.

Developing an Arsenal of Weapons

One of the basic principles of this book is that depending on what kind of anxiety strikes, it's very helpful to be able to target that kind of anxiety with the right kind of technique. We have looked at these in terms of six categories: calming, physical, strengthening, philosophical, practical and medical. In Chapter 2, you learned at least two techniques from each category and completed an Arsenal of Weapons form to remind yourself what techniques you have at your disposal.

In addition, ideally it would be very handy if you had a therapist who knew you and with whom you'd worked, whom you could call and get a couple of appointments with, as and when you need them. This wouldn't work for all kinds of therapy, but could be possible for **Person Centred Therapy**, **Cognitive Behavioral Therapy, REBT** and perhaps **Existential Therapy**. If, when treating the underlying predisposition, you already got a therapist of one of these types, great! They will be able to help you with a flare up when it happens. But if not, give this one some thought. It might be worth finding a therapist of one of the above types and having a couple of sessions to get to know them, even if you're not actually struggling with anxiety right now, so that you can pick up where you left off when you're in the throes of anxiety further down the line.

Undertaking Anxiety-Busting Activities

Regular Anxiety-Busting Activities

If you are a habitual anxiety sufferer, you should do at least one of the following, at least twice a week, but ideally every day:

* Meditation
* Exercise of Any Sort
* Yoga
* Qigong/Tai Chi
* Mindfulness
* Meditation

All of these techniques, or something similar that suits you well, will act to reduce the likelihood of you getting anxiety. The temptation will be for you to let it slide when you're not feeling anxious, but that's the trick: you might avoid the anxiety altogether if you keep doing it when you're OK.

Ad-hoc Anxiety-Busting Activities

It is really useful to develop a mindset where you become aware of what is likely to cause you anxiety, and plan for that anxiety in advance. For example, I have learned that I will often become anxious about large social gatherings. I could be really looking forward to it, without even realising that as the time approaches, the anxiety will start to set in. So, let's say I am going to a friend's wedding in the near future. If I look at it a bit more closely, there would be three elements that might cause me anxiety – my social shyness and having to make small talk with people I don't know, feeling trapped and obliged to stay for a particular length of time, and not having any control over what food and drink is served up to me.

What can I put in place to help me with each of these? For the social shyness, I could, for example, prepare a list of topics that I am going to talk to people about or questions to ask, and learn them off-by-heart. Alternatively, I could set myself a limit of speaking to, say, two strangers, and then restricting the rest of my time to talking to people I do know. Or I could plan to do my inner hero visualisation just before the event, so I know I'll have a strong voice in my head instead of my anxiety voice.

For the feeling trapped part of my anxiety, I could use the One Step at a Time technique, or simply talk to my partner or person I've travelled with and agree a "safe word", something I can say at any point to indicate to them that I've become uncomfortable and need to leave. And for the food and drink anxiety, I could find out in advance what is being served, and if necessary, sneak in something I like to eat and/or drink, so I know I'll have something familiar. I could also plan an explanation in case I am not able to eat what's put in front of me and people choose to discuss it with me.

Based on my example above, mine would be something like this:

Event: Marjorie's wedding

Anxiety Trigger 1: Making small talk with strangers

What I'll do to mitigate or avoid: Prepare a list of topics and questions. Make a limit of two strangers.

Anxiety Trigger 2: Feeling trapped

What I'll do to mitigate or avoid: Use One Step at a Time technique – allow myself to bail out (1) 10 minutes in (2) Straight after ceremony (3) After photos (4) Before reception (5) Straight after meal (6) Straight after speeches.

Anxiety Trigger 3: No control over food and drink

What I'll do to mitigate or avoid: Ask Marjorie for the menu. Take sandwich in handbag.

Monitoring your Anxiety Levels

Keeping an anxiety diary is a good idea for habitual anxiety sufferers. You can do this in any way that you like, and if you don't like too much structure, just a simple (preferably daily) account of your anxiety will do. If you'd prefer to make it a little more organised, one technique is to split it into columns, as I've done in the example on the following page.

---

*Exercise 31 **Anxiety Diary***

Create an anxiety diary like the one on the next page.

Put the date in column 1.
In column 2, describe any worries you felt that day.
In column 3, write any anxiety symptoms that you had.
Then in column 4, the trigger(s) for any anxiety you felt that day. It could be a situation that arose, or a thought, or you might not even know what it is. You might have a suspicion (women for example might consider the time of the month). Or it may simply continue from the previous day.
In the fifth column, give the anxiety a score out of 10, with 10 being the worst anxiety imaginable and 1 being very mild.
In column 6, write anything you tried that day to overcome the anxiety.
In column 7, describe the result of your intervention (you can give "before and after intervention" scores if you prefer).
In column 8, and this is very important, write things you achieved during your day despite having anxiety.

You could then add a free format part for you to make notes about that day's anxiety.

This is very useful for a number of reasons. When you look back over your diary, it will help you to *understand your anxiety better*. It will help you *recognise the symptoms*, so you can use them in the future to help you realise you have anxiety sooner. It will also help you to see *a pattern to what triggers it, what tends to help* and what doesn't. And the last column is important because it shows you that you are not just your anxiety, that it doesn't control you, and that *you still have a positive life despite it*! You'll possibly find there are more days than you realised when your anxiety is absent, or minimal (that's important because we tend to think we live with it constantly).

Date	Worry	Physical & Mental Symptoms	Possible Trigger	Score	Intervention	Result of intervention	Achievements
Aug 6 2018	Worrying about money	Very tired Felt sick Depressed	Hot weather? Stuck in house?	3	Tried breathing exercises	No real effect	Finished photo project. Good evening with friends.
Aug 7 2018	None	Very tired, nausea, shaky	Continued from yesterday	3	Went a walk	Helped reduce	Pushed myself to go a walk even though I didn't want to.
Aug 8 2018	None	None					
Aug 9 2018	None	None					
Aug 10 2018	Anxiety about Dave's party	None	Heard it's going to be a big crowd.	4	None		
Aug 11 2018	Anxiety about party	Lumpy throat, headache	As above	7	Did "inner hero" exercise and breathing exercise.	Really helped, got me through the event	Faced my fears and had a good time at the party.
Aug 12 2018	None	Lumpy throat	Aftermath?	2	3-week rule	Good, reduced as day went on.	Did all the housework!
Aug 13 2018	None	None					

There are disadvantages to keeping a diary though, and it's not for everyone. One is the time commitment – it works best if you do it every day, but having to do it every day might, for a busy person, become another stress. Another thing to consider is that it is making you focus on your anxiety every day. If you believe in the saying "what you focus on, expands", then focussing every day on anxiety might give it more importance than you would otherwise have done. Also, think about the time of day you write it. If you do it just before bed, do you want to go to bed focussed on your anxiety? If you do it in the morning, do you want to start your day focussing on your anxiety? So, whether this technique is a good one for you will depend on your personality and circumstances, but it can be hugely helpful, especially in the first few weeks/months, so do please try it for a while, at different times of day, in order to get to know your anxiety patterns better.

I would suggest that when writing your diary, always go through the Symptoms Checklist as part of the process to help identify hidden anxiety. If you identify anxiety but aren't sure of the cause, you can also go through the Non-worry-based anxiety section in Chapter 3 to help you identify possible reasons. If you have identified a worry that is not very pressing, you can also review the Bogus Worry Checklist Exercise.

Recognising Your Patterns

Every so often, and I'd say at least once a month to begin with, review your diary entries and look at the history of the anxiety you have been suffering. Is there any recurring theme, any pattern as to when and how your anxiety is triggered? *Is there a particular situation, environment, person or group of people that pops up consistently when you have anxiety?* If so, is there something you can do to address this as a potential cause or trigger? Review the sections on Environmental Anxiety, Situational Anxiety and Social Causes in Chapter 5. Likewise, if overload is a common cause of anxiety, review the section on Overload in Chapter 3.

If your anxiety manifests as a worry or worries, *are there any recurring themes or worries?* If so, make a note as to which worry types they belong to, by doing the exercises in Chapter 4. You will then know in advance exactly which techniques you will need to apply if that worry rears its ugly head again. To take my worries from chapter 4 as an example, if I detect that I regularly seem to worry about running out of money, I know from chapter 4 that this (for me) is *low-appropriateness and low-urgency*, and so the best solutions for it will be **Practical Techniques** and **Therapy/Counselling.** Make a note of these repeating worries and the appropriate techniques for treating them.

Also explore whether there is any pattern to the physical symptoms involved in your anxiety. For example, do you often get a bad back, or headache, or dry throat? As I said earlier, recognising these symptoms is very important because they can become early warning signs that you are suffering from anxiety. For health anxiety sufferers, it can also help to quickly diagnose them as anxiety when they happen, rather than causing us to worry they are caused by something more dangerous. Make a note of them.

This all might seem like quite a lot to do, but most of the work will be up front. For example, once you've completed your arsenal of weapons once, you shouldn't have to do it again (except maybe occasionally as a refresher). If you do what's described above regularly, you should find your anxiety reducing, and so you won't be needing to treat your anxiety nearly so often. Recognising your patterns will become much less necessary after the first few weeks.

Nipping it in the Bud

If your monitoring has revealed a current anxiety, then ideally you should work on it straight away. I'm not suggesting, especially for those of us that have many worries, that you work on every single one of them every single time. In fact, depending on what your worry is (if indeed there is a worry), the first thing you could do is to schedule a time for worrying about it later, using the Worry Hour or Three-Week Rule techniques. Use the techniques you've learned to identify the anxiety type and apply the relevant technique(s) to treat it. *You should find that this early recognition and treatment will help to dissipate a bout of anxiety before it takes too strong a hold on you.* You are simply getting out of the area at the first sign that there might be a lion nearby, allowing yourself to quickly return to go-about-your-business mode.

Finally, be sure to *make a note in your anxiety diary of what techniques you tried and whether and how they helped.*

Helping those Around you to Understand and Manage your Anxiety

In The Anxiety Coach in Chapter 2 we looked at how giving someone you trust the tools to help you can be a useful strengthening technique when coping with anxiety. But whether or not you do that, you should also consider talking to those around you to help them understand your anxiety. Hopefully, by doing this, you will:

- Stop them from feeling confused, rejected, frustrated or angry about your behaviour;
- Reduce the chance of them saying or doing the wrong thing;
- Increase the chance of them saying or doing the right thing;
- Reduce the chance of anxiety contagion, by helping them to protect themselves.

In terms of explaining your anxiety, *it's important that people around you understand that anxiety is usually not about the things you are worrying about.* The worries are often just a symptom. As I have said, we all know that we're worrying too much, or sometimes unnecessarily. Knowing that does not mean we can make it go away, because anxiety is not a thought process, it's a physical state, which can be brought about by many things. Let's say you have a neck injury and it hurts when you sneeze or cough. Knowing that you shouldn't sneeze or cough because it will hurt doesn't stop you from doing it, because it's involuntary. Anxiety is also involuntary. *Make sure your loved ones understand this.*

Let them know it's not their job to cheer you up or solve your worries, although there may be times when they can! You don't want them to suffer as well, so it's better for them to just be sympathetic, understanding, supportive and, above all, PATIENT. Remind them that you are not always anxious and that they just have to sit out the storm. Remind them that happy, relaxed you is still in there and that normal service will be resumed as soon as possible.

Help them to not become infected by your anxiety. Suggest to them that when you are having a strong bout, if they also start to feel stressed, they should protect themselves. Perhaps they can imagine themselves in an imaginary spacesuit, as we discussed in Contagion in Chapter 3. Or you could suggest that it's like the safety procedures in an aeroplane: put the oxygen mask on your own face before you try to help others. They need to make sure they aren't breathing in anxiety before they can help you with yours! *Tell them not to get drawn into your "what ifs" or into endless debates with you about what tragedy might be about to occur* (if that's the way you roll). You might also suggest that they themselves learn to use one or two calming and physical techniques in periods when your anxiety levels are high, in order to keep themselves strong. It might even be a nice idea to do some of these techniques together, as a couple or a family for example, when the need arises.

Finally, remember to reassure your loved ones if your anxiety might make them feel insecure. They might feel that you're unhappy in your life, when in fact you're not. It's hard to understand the difference if you don't have Type 2 anxiety. *Reassure them that it's not their fault*, that they are a big help to you, that they make you happy and you love them, it's just a physical problem that can manifest itself as worries and fears.

These ideas have been written with adults in mind, but you should also think about the children in your life and their relationship with your anxiety. Can you explain it to them in simple terms so they can understand? Children growing up around anxiety are more likely to become anxious themselves, so it's better to address it with them than try to hide it from them. It's a difficult subject, but if you can find the right approach, it could be very rewarding.

Dealing with Anxiety Emergencies

Building these routines, warning and support systems will help a huge amount, but we have to acknowledge that there will still be times when anxiety just hits you, hits you hard and knocks you back before you've had a chance to do anything to stop it. Unclear thinking or even panic are part and parcel of anxiety, so it's a really good idea to prepare some sort of "go-to" kit that you reach for when this happens, to remind yourself what to do. Do the exercise on the next page to make an Anxiety SOS Kit that you can use in emergencies.

That's all for Chapter 6. You now have a number of methods for reducing the likelihood of a bout of anxiety, for nipping them in the bud when you do get them, and for reducing the impact they have on your relationships. Our work is done! All that is left now is just to make some final comments and wrap things up.

*Exercise 32 **Making an Anxiety SOS Kit***

In this exercise you're going to make a kit of things you can use when you've got an anxiety emergency. Get a nice box (the size will depend on the contents) and perhaps label it "Anxiety SOS" or something similar.

Put the following things in the box:

(1) Your completed Arsenal of Weapons form. When you open the box, this will instantly remind you what you have at your disposal and stop you from going into a knee-jerk response to what's happening.

(2) Something containing a single motivational saying that you want to remind yourself of when you're caught in the throes of an anxiety emergency. Think a lot about this: what is the one thing that your calm self wants your anxious self to hear at times like this? This could perhaps be just printed on a piece of paper, put inside a little capsule, or printed off on a poster you can pin up somewhere for the day ... whatever works for you.

(3) Depending on what medical weapons you have in your arsenal, you may be able to include these, e.g. a couple of your calming tablets, CBD oil, kava etc.

(4) Include a totem of some sort to complement your strengthening technique. For example, if the Inner Hero technique is in your arsenal, and you chose Captain Kirk as your inspiring figure, you could perhaps put a figurine or photo of him in there.

(5) Anything you'll need for the other weapons. For example, if one of your calming weapons is music and you made a calming music CD or pen drive, put that in the box. If one of the practical weapons is the worry zone or worry-free zone, put some of the props you need for that zone in there (e.g. scented candles, diffused lightbulb, comforting sweater).

(6) A treat for yourself. You're going to be kind to yourself during this battle with anxiety, right? So, let's start by doing something nice for yourself. Put a bar of your favourite chocolate, a sachet of your favourite herbal tea, a cigar or other guilty pleasure in the box.

And there you have it! Your very own Anxiety SOS Kit.

FINAL THOUGHTS

If you've got this far in the book, you've developed skills in six different areas for treating anxiety, you've learned how to identify the type of anxiety you have and the best approach to treating it. You've identified possible reasons for your predisposition to anxiety and the best approaches to treating that predisposition, and you have also put into place a prevention routine that can help you minimise the control it has over your life. Congratulations! I hope you already feel empowered and are able to look at your anxiety more strategically and productively.

In the appendix you'll find more techniques that may be appropriate for each category of technique that we've identified. Space, and my own ignorance, prevent me from including an awful lot of techniques, treatments and therapies that can help with anxiety. Also, many people, including experts, will take issue with some of my interpretations of the ones I have included. The important thing is that *you can use the suggestions here to point you in the right direction and to give you some ideas and inspiration.* You may even redefine the categories themselves; I have identified six (Calming, Physical, Strengthening, Philosophical, Practical and Medical), but you might even discover another, or decide to move mine about a bit to make more sense to you, personally.

How do you know whether the technique is working or not? Well, in some cases, it's obvious; you might know pretty much straight away. In other cases, it will take time, sometimes months, before you can tell. There's an act of faith in some cases. It's often hard to measure whether you're feeling better. Anxiety levels vary naturally, and what's happening in your life, in your head and to your body at any particular time can affect your picture of how you're responding to a technique. Added to that is the fact that there can be a time lag between the anxiety being reduced and you actually feeling the benefit of it, often due to the fact that it takes the body a while to recover from prolonged or intense fight-or-flight (see Aftermath in Chapter 3). Always err on the side of persistence and make sure you give the technique a really good chance of working, before giving up on it and moving to Plan B.

No matter how hard you work on your anxiety, don't be disheartened when it still sometimes gets the better of you. *We all still have bad patches*, myself included. What's important is to recognise that they are fewer and farther between, they don't last as long and they are hopefully less intense than they used to be. Treat every bout as a learning experience and you will continue to refine your anxiety-busting skills.

Remember also the advantages that having Type 2 anxiety can bring. Worriers, by nature, avoid a lot of unnecessary obstacles in life by seeing them coming a mile off, and being able to swerve to avoid them! Anxiety can lead to creativity and inventiveness as we look to respond to a threat. This has all been demonstrated scientifically: research[42] has shown that we are *better than other people* at warning people of danger (of course we are!), that people with social anxiety have *more empathy for others*[43], and that anxiety sufferers are *more intelligent*, on average, than other people[44].

I hope that if nothing else, this book has given you some ideas and skills that you can take forward with you on your journey. I think that knowing and understanding that anxiety is not the same as worrying, that it isn't a thought process but a physical state, is the most important message I want to get across. Why? Because we have to stop focussing purely on the worries and address the condition that is making us worry more than we should. And because we need to address anxiety that has no worry element to it, because it's taking its toll on our body.

Another fundamental message I'd like you to take from this book is "horses for courses". There is no one right way to treat anxiety, because there are many different forms of anxiety. What works brilliantly for some situations can fail miserably in others. I hope the book has helped you to better

---

[42] See for example
http://portal.idc.ac.il/he/schools/psychology/homepage/documents/tsachi-scared%20saviors.pdf
[43] See for example https://doctorsonly.co.il/wp-content/uploads/2011/12/Untitled-Extract-Pages4.pdf
[44] See for example https://www.ncbi.nlm.nih.gov/pmc/articles/PMC3269637/

diagnose the type of anxiety you have, and to be able to apply the best kind of treatment accordingly.

Finally, it's all about management. I'd like to think that as a result of reading this, you are able to know how to avoid bouts of anxiety in the first place and nip them in the bud when they do happen. It should also have helped you to get better support and understanding from those around you, which is vitally important.

Don't forget to pick the book up again regularly for a bit of revision, and to make this book your first port of call when you experience bouts of anxiety in the future. If you'd like to work directly with me to put the ideas from this book into practice in your life, please look at details of the Anxiety Workshop in Appendix C for information on the coaching I offer. Finally, I'd love to receive suggestions and feedback for later editions. My contact details are also included in Appendix C.

Thank you for reading and good luck in your own personal battle with anxiety!

Appendix A: FURTHER TECHNIQUES AND TREATMENTS

More Calming Techniques

Guided Imagery

Guided imagery is a technique where you are invited to imagine yourself in a particular situation. It can often very successfully be used simply as a relaxation technique. You can buy, stream or download recordings of a voice that, for example, tells you to imagine yourself on a tropical beach, or peaceful meadow and which guides you through the scene you are visualizing. Usually this is done in a quiet place with your eyes closed, but it can also be while focussing on a buddha, or a candle, or even a photo of the relaxing place. The process usually also includes breathing techniques as discussed above. Guided imagery is also a technique used in meditation (see below), so it overlaps with that. It is another way of turning off your fight-or-flight mode, a bit like method acting, where, by imagining yourself to be in this peaceful situation, your nervous system will respond accordingly and take you off alert.

This is something you can try yourself. You can find scripts on the internet, record them yourself or download an audio file of someone reading it. There are plenty of websites that offer recordings (some are free, others are paid) and/or ready-made scripts for you to record yourself, and you can also make your own.

Some of the many websites offering guided imagery for relaxation and calmness are:
http://www.innerhealthstudio.com/visualization-scripts.html
https://www.guidedimagerydownloads.com
https://www.relaxforawhile.com/guided-relaxation-gallery.html
http://www.meditatia.com/guided-meditation-anxiety.html

Alternatively, there are therapists who work with guided imagery in a much more involved way, some of whom might argue that for guided imagery to be effective, you have to do far more than shut your eyes and listen to a script. There is quite a developed set of skills and tools involved. The Wikipedia entry on guided imagery reflects this more involved approach: *"Guided imagery (also known as Guided Affective Imagery, or KIP, Katathym-imaginative Psychotherapy) is a mind-body intervention by which a trained practitioner or teacher helps a participant or patient to evoke and generate mental images that simulate or re-create the sensory perception of sights, sounds, tastes, smells, movements, and images associated with touch, such as texture, temperature, and pressure, as well as imaginative or mental content that the participant or patient experiences as defying conventional sensory categories, and that may precipitate strong emotions or feelings in the absence of the stimuli to which correlating sensory receptors are receptive."*

In other words, using our imagination to simulate the senses, which will stimulate the brain to respond to the imaginary situation. If you are drawn to this technique and are able to visit a specialist practitioner, you'll be getting the Rolls Royce version of the guided imagery technique.

Guided imagery is also used for many things besides relaxation, in the treatment of phobias for example, when you would imagine yourself confronting the object of your fear. You can also be guided to imagine empowering situations where you are brave and overcome your fear. I talk about this aspect in the more strengthening techniques section, below. But in terms of this section, calming techniques, look simply for guided imagery that helps you to relax.

Guided imagery can be particularly useful when performed last thing before bed, or if you wake up in the middle of the night, to help you to a better sleep.

Meditation

This is something I've never been able to master fully myself but if you can do it, it will probably be a great benefit to you in general, not just when you need to relax and come out of fight-or-flight. There are many different forms of meditation, but in terms of meditation 101, you need only to follow a few simple steps, such as in the exercise below.

1. Sit with a straight back
You can practice meditation while standing, walking, lying or even running, so I'm told, but normally it is done sitting. I am not sure why the cross-legged position on the floor, or on a cushion, is seen as the ideal, but if you can sit comfortably that way with a straight back, do so. Otherwise sit in a chair, or on a stool, wherever you are comfortable and where your back is straight. Imagine a string coming out of the top of your head and pulling you upward toward the ceiling to help you to sit tall and straight.

2. Breathe deeply
Close your eyes and start to use a deep breathing technique such as I described in Chapter 2. Try to imagine breathing the air deep into your belly.

3. Relax your muscles
Follow around your body in your mind, relaxing each body part one at a time. Sometimes it helps to tense the muscle first before letting it go. Begin with your toes and feet and work upward.

4. Repeat a mantra
A mantra is a sound, word or phrase that is repeated throughout your meditation. It provides a point of focus during meditation and helps to suppress your wandering mind. If you get into meditation from a spiritual point of view, mantras can also have some meaning. But for now, as a relaxation method, your mantra can simply be saying with each breath, aloud or in your head, *breathing in, breathing out*.

5. Be present and calm
The combination of 1-4 should help your mind to empty and for you to feel more peaceful in the here-and-now. Now they say, as thoughts come to you, simply acknowledge them, set them aside, and return your attention to your mantra. That's the bit where it falls down for me! But don't beat yourself up if you're like me and you can't stop that constant chatter. Keep at it and hopefully it will get easier. Also note there is still value in the meditation even if your mind is chattering all the way through!

6. Ending
When you first start, try just 5 or 10 minutes, but you can work yourself up to longer periods. When you're ready to finish, start to slowly stretch or wiggle your fingers, toes, wrists, ankles, gently turn or twist your shoulders, neck and hips, open your eyes and bring yourself back into your day.

Further steps with Meditation

Don't be like me and give up with meditation. It takes time, commitment and practice before you start to feel the true benefits. Once you have this basic technique mastered, if you are finding it helpful, there is a whole world of meditation out there for you to develop into. There is an excellent webpage at https://liveanddare.com/types-of-meditation that introduces 23 of the most established forms of meditation, so you can pick one that best suits you. You might also want to check out the work of Sam Harris[45].

Finally, a beautiful tool that aids meditation and promotes relaxation is the singing bowl. These bowls have been used for centuries in Buddhist circles both for healing in their own right, and as a kind of signal booster for getting into a meditative state. They can also be a very pretty ornament to have around the house! Find out more at https://jevondangeli.com/tibetan-singing-bowls-the-ancient-brain-entrainment-methodology-for-healing-and-meditation/

EFT/Tapping

The "Emotional Freedom Technique" or EFT or "Tapping" is a technique that uses the body's energy meridian points, like acupuncture. The idea is that instead of using needles or acupressure, these same meridian points can be stimulated by tapping on them with your fingertips. It is relatively simple to learn the basic points and apply this technique to ease your anxiety. I don't have much personal experience of this and there is not a great deal of scientific evidence as to its effectiveness, but I have certainly known people who have benefitted from it. If you try it and find it useful, please let me know. More information can be found at:

https://www.emofree.com/nl/eft-tutorial/tapping-basics/how-to-do-eft.html

Use some of the physical techniques as well

Most physical approaches also have a calming effect, so when you are looking for a calming technique, consider also physical ones. In particular, consider Massage, Progressive Muscle Relaxation, Yoga and Qigong/Tai Chi.

---

[45] See www.samharris.org

Other Calming Techniques

There are many other things that fit in to the calming category that will work for some people better than for others. Aromatherapy, for example, is found by some people to be very relaxing. Getting out and about in nature can help, as can rescue remedies, painting or colouring in, doing sudokus, or stroking a pet. If you have possible environmental anxiety, it might sound obvious, but try to avoid or limit your exposure to the possibly anxiety-provoking environment. Or, if you think you might have seasonal affective disorder (SAD), some sunshine and light – real or artificially produced, might be a good place to start. Some people find that smiling or laughter therapy can be a useful way of getting yourself out of fight-or-flight ... you might feel silly doing it, but if it works, it might be worth the embarrassment! Think about things that relax you and try to bring them, or something similar, into your daily life.

More Physical Techniques

Dancing

As I've discussed, music has an extremely powerful effect on mood and can be very effective in combating anxiety. As I've also discussed, exercise has an extremely powerful effect on mood and can be very effective in combating anxiety. Dancing – bringing the two of them together – has got to be a winner, then, hasn't it? Any kind of dancing is good, but in some ways, the best thing to do is to combine dancing with either very relaxing or very energetic, emotional music, as I talked about in the section on music in Chapter 2 - do it on your own behind closed doors so you don't feel self-conscious if you like. Move to the music in any way that comes to you. Don't let anyone shame you and just give it a try.

If you find this helps and want to take it further, you can try dancercise, dance classes, or you could consider dance movement therapy, which is a psychotherapy that uses dance and movement in a holistic mind-body approach[46].

---

[46] See for example https://en.wikipedia.org/wiki/Dance_therapy for more details.

Qigong/Tai Chi

Studies have consistently shown the benefits of qigong or tai chi in the treatment of anxiety[47]. These two Chinese disciplines are very similar. Qigong focusses on developing and directing the Qi, or Chi, which according to Chinese philosophy and medicine is the life force that circulates around our body. Tai Chi, although related, is basically a martial art, so it contains elements of attack and defence within its postures. Qigong/Tai Chi is based on slow, gentle physical movement, so it is less physically demanding than yoga and more suitable for people who find exercise difficult.

See https://www.qigonginstitute.org/category/4/getting-started for more information.

Progressive Muscle Relaxation

Progressive Muscle Relaxation is a technique designed to combat anxiety, in which you systematically tense and then relax the muscles around your body. It is easy to learn, is supported by plenty of scientific evidence and has the advantage of being able to be applied absolutely anywhere and at any time. There is an excellent guide at
https://www.anxietybc.com/sites/default/files/MuscleRelaxation.pdf.

Massage

Scientific evidence as to massage's effectiveness in reducing anxiety is surprisingly mixed, as it would seem a naturally stress-relieving thing to do. Certainly at a physical level, it should at the very least *release tension from a number of muscle groups, thereby lowering the physical symptoms of anxiety and promoting relief.* Perhaps, among other things, scientific research has been complicated by the many different types of massage available. Some are more geared toward injuries (for example, sports massage, deep tissue massage, neuromuscular therapy) and some toward promoting energy (for example, Thai massage, Shiatsu). The types that are probably best for anxiety are the *traditional Swedish massage, hot stone massages and perhaps foot massages.* Also, the individual skills of the masseur do vary widely, with some using therapeutic aids (such as electric massagers) etc., some using aromatherapy, some opting for gentler and

---

[47] See for example https://www.ncbi.nlm.nih.gov/pmc/articles/PMC3917559/

others more rigorous kneading, and so on. Find a masseur that feels right for you, and don't be afraid to try a few, because it's a very personal choice.

More Strengthening Techniques

Strengthening Guided Imagery

In More Calming Techniques I described the use of guided imagery to find relaxation and take us out of fight-or-flight. But guided imagery can also be used to help us find strength so we can tackle the situation head on. Look for scripts and or classes that can do this as an alternative, for example at https://www.innerhealthstudio.com/visualization-scripts.html. This works very well in conjunction with the exercise Developing your Inner Demon and Inner Hero.

Strengthening Meditation

Likewise, in More Calming Techniques I described the use of meditation in to find relaxation and take us out of fight-or-flight. But meditation can also be used to help us find strength so we can tackle the situation head on, it can also help us to find meaning in what we are feeling, focus on finding solutions, live in the here-and-now (instead of worrying about tomorrow) and/or simply finding acceptance.

Reiki

According to Reiki.org, "Reiki is a Japanese technique for stress reduction and relaxation that also promotes healing. It is administered by 'laying on hands' and is based on the idea that an unseen 'life force energy' flows through us and is what causes us to be alive. If one's 'life force energy' is low, then we are more likely to get sick or feel stress, and if it is high, we are more capable of being happy and healthy."

I've never really connected with Reiki and have felt a little sceptical about it, but I'm including it here because I have known a number of people who do get a lot of benefit from it and practice it as part of their daily lives. Find out more at https://www.reiki.org/faq/whatisreiki.html

More Philosophical Techniques

Simple Philosophical Reminders

When you are anxious, it is sometimes helpful to simply sit somewhere quietly and remind yourself of some very basic truths. Here are some examples: "Life is very short", "I could be dead tomorrow", "You only live once (YOLO)", "We regret the things we haven't done rather than those we have done", "This, too, will pass", "What doesn't kill me makes me stronger", "I have enough, I am enough", "I can live a full and happy life, even with my anxiety". Some people find it helpful to sit and say, "I'm thankful for …" and then list all the things they can think of that fit that particular bill.

We all know some of these "Truisms" and pithy sayings, and you might be pretty sceptical about them. In modern society, we tend to be bombarded by these sayings – on Facebook, clothes, ornaments and furniture, for example. And I certainly don't want some chirpy, annoying Type 1's and 3's quoting them at me when I'm in anxiety mode. But the fact that they've been popularised, and let's face it, trivialised, doesn't make them any less true in essence. The important thing is to *identify those that are relevant and personal to you and the anxiety you are suffering.*

---

*Exercise 34 **Simple Philosophical Reminders***

Choose three sayings that can inspire you to face your current anxiety. If the suggestions I've made above don't quite float your boat, find suggestions on the internet[48], or you can make your own.

Write them on the bathroom mirror or stick them on a note on the back of the living room door, or inside your desk drawer at work – wherever you think you'll need reminding of them. If this method is useful to begin with but then loses its power, think of changing the three expressions for different ones every now and then.

At the time in my life when my anxiety was at it's very worst, I found three expressions that really worked for me at the time. I used to work on my

---

[48] See for example https://www.briantracy.com/blog/personal-success/26-motivational-quotes-for-success/

laptop a lot, so I made a screensaver from them, so I'd see them several times a day. They were:

- *You are alive and functioning today. Celebrate that!* (A good one for people with health anxiety.)
- *Choose not to feel the fear.* (This can be seen as putting your inner hero in charge, instead of your inner demon.)
- *Do something nice for someone.* I talk about this more in Turning Outward/Helping Others in Chapter 2 – this is a subtle yet extremely effective cognitive realignment.

Religion, Faith, Belief System

If you don't have a faith, this obviously won't be useful for you – you can't make yourself believe something, even if you knew that believing in it would give you comfort. But if you do have a faith, remember to use it! Go to your church, mosque, temple or meeting room, talk to your pastor or guru or priest. Pray in whatever way your faith tells you to pray. Your faith gives meaning to your suffering and can really help you to overcome your anxiety. Your God or Gods will listen.

Without being religious or believing in a God as such, you may still have a belief system that sustains you and gives your life meaning. For example, I have a belief that I find impossible to explain properly, but which is basically that time does not really exist, and that we live every moment of our lives kind of in the same instant, or for eternity – neither of which are strictly true as time doesn't exist (I get myself in a muddle trying to explain it). In relation to my anxiety, it is a big help for me when I remind myself of it, because it tells me that being in the here-and-now is all that matters, and it reminds me to get back here. I'm not suggesting you try to get your head around my personal belief, but if you have something similar, some sort of explanation for life and what it's all about, use it to help you with your anxiety.

It seems strange to say it, but *we forget to access our belief systems when we are anxious*, and we need to remind ourselves to focus on them, to allow them to help us.

Mindfulness

Mindfulness is a kind of meditation and very compatible with yoga. According to the Greater Good Magazine (https://greatergood.berkeley.edu/topic/mindfulness/definition)

"Mindfulness means maintaining a moment-by-moment awareness of our thoughts, feelings, bodily sensations, and surrounding environment, through a gentle, nurturing lens.

Mindfulness also involves acceptance, meaning that we pay attention to our thoughts and feelings without judging them—without believing, for instance, that there's a "right" or "wrong" way to think or feel in a given moment. When we practice mindfulness, our thoughts tune into what we're sensing in the present moment rather than rehashing the past or imagining the future."

This excellent approach crosses over between the Calming category, the Strengthening category and the Philosophical category. There are countless examples of mindfulness exercises on the Internet, for a very simple introduction I would recommend https://www.pocketmindfulness.com/6-mindfulness-exercises-you-can-try-today/.

More Practical Techniques

The Worry Zone and the Worry-Free Zone

A similar technique to the Worry Hour is the Worry Zone. Rather than being anxious everywhere you go, you allocate a place – a room in your house, under a tree in your garden, the backseat of your car – where you will do all your worrying. As with the worry hour, if you find yourself worrying anywhere else, you remind yourself that you are not in the right place for doing so. You can make your Worry Zone a safe haven, away from distractions.

Of course, you can even combine the Worry Hour with the Worry Zone and enjoy the benefits of both!

I have also heard of people using the reverse technique, i.e. having a "worry-free zone", where if they find themselves worrying, they remind themselves that they are not allowed to do so in that place. Again, this place could be a calm, quiet, soothing, safe place.

One Step at a Time

If the thing that's causing you anxiety involves a period of time that you have to endure or a process that you have to go through, then it's an excellent idea to break it down into stages and, if possible, to allow yourself to take it one step at a time. For example, let's say you are anxious about going on a date. Set the first goal as getting ready to go out. Say to yourself, I'm just going to get ready to go out. That's my goal. If then I decide not to go out, it's OK. Once ready, the next step might be getting to the meeting place. You say to yourself, I'm just going to the meeting place. If I decide not to go in, that's OK. If you get there, you can then set yourself the goal of just going in and spending 5 minutes on the date. If after that 5 minutes you don't want to carry on, you give yourself permission to make a polite excuse and leave, and so on.

By breaking it down in this way, you don't have to push yourself too far or commit to too much up front, and so you can just play it by ear and respond according to how far your comfort levels are able to go.

Even if it's a situation where you can't bail out at various points, it can still be very valuable to mentally break it down into stages and give yourself a little check and pat on the back as you hit each milestone. Sometimes being able to say to yourself, "3 steps down, just 3 to go", for example, makes any process seem less daunting. You might even want to offer yourself rewards for each step that you manage to get through.

Keeping Busy/Distraction

Just because this solution is obvious, doesn't mean it's not worth mentioning. If you have worry-anxiety, distracting yourself from your worries can give you some much-needed respite from fight-or-flight. Try to make yourself spend time with other people, even when you really don't want to. It will help. Do something, some activity, a social event is perfect, and/or things involving using your brain and body - games or sports, or just something interactive, such as a pub quiz or game of cards. Even going to the cinema is good, even though you might feel it's the same as watching a movie at home. It isn't. It's something that is getting you out of the house, and therefore to some extent, out of your own head, and, if you go with someone, it's going to help you focus on other people a little. In addition, all the actions you need to take in order to get to the cinema and come home from it can help to bring you into the here-and-now, even if you're going to see a sci-fi movie!

Learn new techniques and exercises

This book can only scratch the surface of all the possible approaches to anxiety that may exist out there. One thing you can always do to help fight your anxiety is to research new techniques. *Try something different.* Read other self-help books or get some REBT or CBT type therapy (see below) where you are given homework and encouraged to try new approaches. Google™ what helps with anxiety and see what other people suggest or join online forums and share experiences of different techniques with other people. You could even do what I'm doing here and write a book about how to deal with anxiety. This research can be therapeutic in itself, because it can distract you from your worries and encourage you forward. And if you do uncover or develop a new technique, you'll feel really empowered.

Just Do It

You know, depending on the cause of your worry, you might just be able to say "To hell with it, I'm just going to do it and get it over with". Springing that decision on yourself can be great, because it doesn't give you time to stress any more about it. Let's say you have been getting yourself into a state about ringing to get your exam results, or you're going to put your house on the market, or you need to have that difficult conversation that you've been dreading. Ask yourself, can I do it, now, this minute? If you can, do. Whatever happens as a result may or may not cause you to worry, but at least you'll have moved forward. This is similar to the Choose Fight or Flight Technique, but the difference here is that this is an instantaneous, snap decision to fight. Yes or no – now.

Other Medical Approaches

Acupuncture

Acupuncture may be able to help with anxiety. It is a practice from Eastern medicine that involves a professional inserting needles into pressure points on your body (acupressure uses the same points, but just applies pressure instead of inserting needles). The clinical evidence is limited, but promising,[49] in regard to its effectiveness in treating anxiety. In the past, a lot of studies have been criticised for being poorly designed or not having enough participants. However, quite a few stronger studies over the past few years have found good evidence that acupuncture can, in fact, modify the triggering of the fight-or-flight mechanism, so it is certainly an avenue worth exploring if you are looking for a medical approach to treating your anxiety.

Adaptogenic herbs

I have to confess that I had never heard of adaptogens until doing research for this book, but there is a rapidly growing body of research[50] around these plants and their effects on fight-or-flight.

Developed from research during World War II that aimed to find substances that could improve the performance of pilots, the term "adaptogen" is used to describe properties of plants that increase the body's resistance to anxiety by strengthening the adrenal system.

Adaptogenic herbs are not a specific family of plants, but rather a term used to describe any herbs that have these adaptogenic properties. Some of the most popular adaptogenic herbs are schisandra, eleutherococcus (Siberian ginseng), rhodiola, ashwagandha, holy basil and maca.

They each work in different ways – for example, ashwagandha is reported to have a strengthening and soothing effect, rhodiola is believed to combat

---

[49] See for example https://www.ncbi.nlm.nih.gov/pubmed/17641561
[50] See for example https://www.ncbi.nlm.nih.gov/pmc/articles/PMC3991026/

fatigue that is caused by anxiety, Siberian ginseng is claimed to be mood enhancing, and maca is believed to moderate anxiety and support hormonal balance.

There is an excellent introduction to adaptogens at https://www.wellandgood.com/good-advice/adaptogens-explained.

Other herbal remedies

Valerian offers one of the best-studied herbal alternatives for treating anxiety. Although, again, research is mixed, there is enough evidence to at least suggest that it might help with anxiety, with few reported side effects. It is also used as a sleeping aid and one drawback of its use in combatting anxiety is that it can cause some people to feel drowsy.

Passionflower (or passiflora) is another promising herb which has performed well in recent trials[51]. It is often combined with valerian. Other herbs found to have a good effect in treating anxiety include kava (although there have been scare stories about its effects on the liver), chamomile (usually taken as a tea) and lavender (often taken by means of aromatherapy, using lavender oil).

---

[51] See for example
https://www.gaiaherbs.com/uploads/A_Research_Review_of_Passionflower-1371567390.pdf

Appendix B. PSYCHOTHERAPY AND COUNSELLING

There are hundreds of different types or "schools" of psychotherapy[52]. They may all offer help for the anxiety sufferer and I don't pretend to know enough to judge many of them one way or another. What I aim to do here is to discuss some of the most mainstream schools that are, on the surface of it at least, likely to be able to help with different types of anxiety.

Cognitive Behavioural Therapy (CBT)

The aim of Cognitive Behavioural Therapy (CBT) is to help the client think and behave in more positive and productive ways. Rather than focusing on how you feel, which can be hard to change, the premise is that if you change the way you think and behave, which should be easier to do, you will start to feel differently as well. CBT is (usually) a short-term type of therapy that is used to treat a wide range of issues, including anxiety. You will hear it described as "evidence-based" and it is generally favoured by the NHS in the UK over other forms of therapy. Both of these facts are interconnected – it tends to be used to address a specific issue (panic attacks, phobias etc) and because of this and because it's short term, it is much cheaper than other forms of therapy and it is much easier to study its effectiveness (because it's easier to measure: before CBT, the person had an extreme fear of flying, now, the fear is only mild, for example). So being "evidence-based" doesn't mean it's better or more scientific than any other type. Choose it because it's the right approach for your anxiety and not because of cost or because of being impressed by words like "evidence-based".

In terms of the causes of anxiety, CBT will work particularly well for hereditary, phobic and metaphobic types. Hereditary anxiety can be as much (or more) about how we're brought up to think than about genetic factors, so *CBT's ability to help us change the way we think can be invaluable*. Likewise, it may be of help in dealing with historic anxiety. In terms of phobias, it can work at both a thinking level (helping you to think more positively and challenge "faulty thinking") and at a behavioural level (using techniques such as *exposure therapy* and *desensitization* to overcome a fear).

---

[52] See https://en.wikipedia.org/wiki/List_of_psychotherapies

In terms of addressing anxiety symptoms, it is *particularly useful in low immediacy situations*, but arguably can be applied just about anywhere (even in high immediacy situations, if the tools have already been learned).

For more information on CBT and anxiety, see
https://www.anxietybc.com/what-cbt-1.

Rational Emotive Behaviour Therapy (REBT)

Rational Emotive Behaviour Therapy (REBT) is sometimes described as a type of CBT, because it also works at the cognitive and behavioural levels, but it has some important differences from other forms of CBT, including a philosophical element and the inclusion of emotional aspects, which CBT tends to disregard. "Why is this important?" I hear you ask. Well, arguably, and depending on the person and situation, *REBT may be a lot more useful to people who suffer more generalized anxiety than CBT*. This is because while CBT will challenge your thinking on a particular subject, REBT will *challenge your core beliefs*.

REBT says we make demands, on ourselves, other people and the world, that are unrealistic. Anxiety stems from the fact that we believe that our demand must be fulfilled and that it will be awful if it isn't. REBT therefore challenges this "musterbating" (demanding that things "must" happen) and "awfulising" (believing it will be awful if the thing didn't happen) and gives the client tools and techniques to challenge this form of thinking in whatever situation might arise.

Let's say the client is anxious about having to give a speech at a wedding, feeling he will be nervous, stumble over his words, be laughed at and ruin the wedding. CBT would tend to ask questions such as "can you think of a similar situation when you did well and nobody laughed and you didn't ruin everything?", "what might people like about you when you're standing there giving that speech?" etc. In other words, helping him to think more positively and believe that he can do it. REBT, on the other hand, helps the client to see that he is making demands ("I demand that I deliver a good speech", "I demand that it goes well", etc). Can you demand that happens? No. But by demanding it, you are placing inappropriate pressure on yourself, which creates anxiety.

REBT will also adopt what I call the Dr Peppers approach. "What's the worst thing that can happen?" If it's ruining the wedding, "Is that really AWFUL? Is it really a CATASTROPHE?" REBT says, it might be bad if that happened, but it wouldn't be the end of the world. From "I must deliver a great speech and it must go well, otherwise I'll ruin the wedding" (a very anxiety provoking headful of thoughts!) we get to something like "It would be nice, but not essential, that I deliver a good speech and that it goes well, but if I don't, or it doesn't, then it wouldn't be the end of the world as we know it" (a much less anxiety-provoking headful of thoughts.)

What's more, your REBT therapist will teach you to apply those sorts of challenges to any situation, so you *become your own therapist*. This is why it may be particularly useful for people with generalized anxiety, or with a number of different anxieties.

In terms of causes, REBT is also very useful for hereditary and metaphobic anxieties, for similar reasons to CBT, above. In addition, REBT may be an excellent choice for situational anxiety (by challenging the "musts" and "awfuls"). There is also some evidence that it is useful in treating PTSD and therefore also historic anxiety.

In terms of current worries, it can work with most types, although for the high immediacy types, the techniques would have had to have already been learned by the client and self-applied in the heat of the moment (obviously there is no time to have a series of sessions.)

Person-Centred Therapy (PCT)

The idea of person-centred therapy or counselling is that it is client-led. The therapist doesn't come in with any preconceived ideas or theories, except that she must offer genuineness, empathy and unconditional positive regard to the client. Given these "core conditions", the client will be able to express herself, flourish and find the solutions to her own issues.

In terms of anxiety, person-centred therapy is perhaps unlikely to resolve the cause or symptoms of anxiety (although it is certainly possible). However, it should usually be beneficial in terms of having a safe space to explore all the issues around your anxiety, having a sounding board, letting off steam and feeling less embarrassed, ashamed and/or alone with the problem. It will usually *start to help from day one* and continue as long as you need it, or as and when you need it. It's therefore applicable to pretty much all causes and symptoms.

Psychodynamic Therapy

Psychodynamic therapy is an umbrella term that describes a lot of different schools of therapy, for example, Freudian psychoanalysis, Adlerian, Kleinian, Jungian and Eriksonian (and more generic and eclectic forms of these). It generally involves a *therapist-led systematic investigation* into the psychological motivations that underpin your behaviour, thoughts and emotions. It is thought that most of these motivations are *based on early (usually childhood) experiences* and that most are *unconscious*. By exploring childhood memories, along with the client's dreams and other manifestations of his unconscious mind, the therapist encourages the client to make the unconscious conscious, helping him to understand why he is the way he is, and allowing him to have more control over his impulses, behaviour and relationships.

By nature, psychodynamic therapy usually takes a long time, often years. It's therefore not really appropriate to treating the symptoms of anxiety (although talking to your therapist can always have a cathartic effect), but it can really come into its own when dealing with historic causes or unknown or unconscious causes (for obvious reasons). It can also sometimes help with situational causes, as long as they're not too immediate, as it can help you to understand your own behaviour in that situation and potentially allow you to change it. It can also help with phobic anxieties, in that the phobia can be an unconscious, adaptive behaviour relating to repressed trauma.

Psychodynamic therapy is a huge commitment but can be very rewarding in terms of increased self-awareness, and arguably has the greatest potential to improve chronic, historical anxiety.

Existential Therapy

Existential therapy offers a completely different way of looking at anxiety. It is based on the so-called "existential" philosophies of the likes of Nietzsche, Kierkegaard, Sartre, Camus and Heidegger, which, (at the risk of a rather extreme over-simplification), fundamentally argue that existence is meaningless, that each person is fundamentally alone and that death is inevitable. These facts, along with what Kierkegaard called "the dizziness of freedom", or the responsibility placed upon us by the fact that we have free will, by their very nature create anxiety. Therefore, according to existential thinking, anxiety is pretty much our natural state of being. *Those who are not anxious are in denial!*

Now in terms of treating anxiety, you can look at this in two ways. First, that existential therapy sounds utterly terrifying and the last thing that an anxiety sufferer needs to go near. But the flip side of this is interesting. First, it tells you that it is *normal and natural to be anxious*. That can be a big help to those of us that beat ourselves up for being anxious, who wish we could be different, or who feel stupid or a failure because of it. It is empowering.

Second, it tells you that *anxiety is unavoidable*. This can be a very powerful message because it helps us to stop fighting against our anxiety, and to accept it. As I've discussed already above, when it comes to anxiety, most of our energy is spent battling with it, and just accepting it – saying "OK anxiety, you're not a pleasant feeling, but I have to live with you" can paradoxically make it seem so much less potent, and sometimes fall away altogether (see Acceptance).

The third interesting aspect is that *this approach will explain your anxiety better than any other*. The "why am I feeling so anxious?" question is finally answered. Let's take that guy who has to give the speech at the wedding. An existential therapist will help him to drill down and see that fear of humiliation or of ruining the wedding as something else. Why is it scary to be laughed at or ridiculed? Maybe because you feel alone and separated from all those around you (because they are "against" you in that moment). It speaks to our *existential aloneness*. The therapist may also relate the anxiety to that of freedom – that the speaker is totally in control of his own words, his own mouth, his own performance – and so making this speech speaks to his existential freedom and the responsibility that goes with it. The anxiety felt with this situation may also speak to anxiety about his *mortality* – that a disaster or failure is like a mini-death and therefore triggers existential dread (or fear of death).

In terms of causes, existential therapy may therefore be particularly useful in dealing with situational, phobic and metaphobic, PTSD and unconscious or unknown types. In terms of current worries, those with *high severity* and *low immediacy* may benefit from an existential approach.

It is a gamble, and exposure to this type of approach may of course make your anxiety worse. If you do want to give it a try, before starting therapy, talk to the therapist in detail about your struggles with anxiety and how this can be managed during the process.

Hypnotherapy

Hypnotherapy uses hypnosis to treat psychological issues. One of its key features is that it requires the client to reach very deep levels of relaxation and so *by its very nature, it can help to reduce anxiety*, at least, at the time of the treatment and for a short while after. When used to treat anxiety, it can help the client to focus clearly on whatever is the cause of the anxiety, and to develop self-suggestive techniques to find strength and cope with the anxiety-provoking situation, as I discussed above in Strengthening Techniques. In theory, hypnosis can be used to turn off the fight-or-flight mechanism and the client can also be given the ability to call upon the suggestions provided by the therapist in anxiety provoking situations. Let's take the example of a person who becomes very anxious when flying. First, the therapist will induce a fully relaxed state in the client. This is the state in which we are most susceptible to suggestion. The therapist might then invite the client to see himself boarding an aeroplane with confidence, experiencing turbulence and knowing it is OK, and so on. Finally, the therapist might give the client keywords (such as "calm and confident") or a technique (such as tapping the back of his left hand three times with his right index finger) by which this state of strength and non-anxiety can be summoned.

Hypnotherapy is *particularly appropriate to phobic and metaphobic types of anxiety and PTSD,* but may be useful in all types. It is also theoretically appropriate to most, if not all types of current worry, once the client becomes able to summon the coping state in himself.

The success of hypnotherapy to a great extent will come down to your "suggestibility". Some people are more suggestible than others (basically, they can be hypnotised more easily). For others, the effect is more diluted and not powerful enough to overcome their anxiety, especially when the degree of terror is high.

Art and Performance therapies

Talking therapies are not for everyone, and sometimes we find it hard to express in words anxiety that we feel. It is always worth bearing in mind that there are other forms of therapy that might help us to identify, express or come to terms with our anxiety in a different way. For example, *art therapy* uses art media as the primary form of expressing yourself. There are many different forms of art therapy (or you could see it as there being an art therapy version of most types of talking therapy: psychoanalytic art therapy, person-centred art therapy and so on). There are two aspects to art therapy: one is for the client to *express herself in a creative way that isn't restricted by language*, which in itself can be cathartic (this is the more person-centred approach); the other is for therapist and client to *analyse* the art produced by the client in order to provide insights into the client's unconscious (the more psychodynamic approach).

Another form of therapy that can help in dealing with anxiety is *Dramatherapy*. This will encourage you to play different characters in different scenarios. Dramatherapy offers eight different mechanisms, such as *dramatic projection* – a technique that allows the client to "project" her emotions onto a role she is playing in order to work out her issues (in our case, her worries); *Personification and impersonation* – where the client expresses her own issues through the character she is portraying; and *Dramatherapeutic empathy and distancing* – where the client can perform material (roles, plays, stories) that resonates with her personal issues.

Music and dance therapy are other forms of non-talking therapies.

These sorts of therapies can be great for *traumatic reasons for predisposition*, that is, either historic or PTSD. In terms of current anxiety, they lend themselves particularly well to *high terror* worries.

Couples, family or relationship counselling

If your anxiety might be caused or worsened by a relationship or social issue such as those described in Social Causes in Chapter 5, or indeed if your anxiety is negatively affecting a relationship, then you could consider having relationship counselling with the person or people involved. These take many different forms and will usually follow one of the schools of therapy described above (e.g. psychodynamic, person-centred, CBT).

Appendix C. THE ANXIETY WORKSHOP and FEEDBACK

The Anxiety Workshop

If you'd like to work directly with me to implement the ideas presented in this book, please visit my website at anxiety-self-help.co.uk for information about The Anxiety Workshop. This is a one-to-one Skype-based course of six one-hour sessions. My website also contains up-to-date contact information and details of my other books.

Feedback and Contact

We are all in the battle against anxiety together and I'm sure I can learn as much from you as you can from me. Please send me feedback on the book, what you liked, what you didn't like, what you think I've missed out, and any useful ideas, techniques and strategies you have come across in your own personal battle. Please visit my website at the address shown above for my up-to-date contact details. Thank you!

Index of Exercises

Index of Techniques

Thanks to everyone who has helped to make this book possible; to everyone who has given me advice and feedback on the content; to those who have designed, helped with and given feedback on the cover and titles; to everyone who has helped to spread the word and promote it, and those who have simply supported and encouraged me; and most of all, to Shaz.

Printed in Great Britain
by Amazon